This book is dedicated to Mary and Tasha, my best
friends and partners; and to my parents, Margaret and
David, who early on instilled in me a love of history,
travel, and adventure.

Page 1: Maneuvering a canoe in Maine's Allagash River
Pages 2–3: Southern Utah caprocks
Page 4: Northern New England forest engulfed in fog

First published in the United States of America in 1999
by UNIVERSE PUBLISHING
A Division of Rizzoli International Publications, Inc.
300 Park Avenue South, New York, NY 10010

Library of Congress Cataloging-in-Publication Data

Gorman, Stephen.
        The American wilderness : journeys into
    distant and historic landscapes / photography
    and text by Stephen Gorman ; foreword by
    David Quammen.
                p.   cm.
    ISBN 0–7893–0273–X (hard : alk. paper). —
    ISBN 0–7893–0274–8 (pbk. : alk. paper)
        1. United States—Description and travel.
    2. United States—Pictorial works. 3. Wilderness
    areas—United States. 4. Gorman, Stephen—
    Journeys—United States. 5. Wilderness areas—
    United States—Guidebooks. I. Title.
    E169.04.G66   1999
    917.3'0022'2—DC21   99–17147
                                         CIP

Design and typography by Russell Hassell

Printed in Singapore

99 00 01 02 / 10 9 8 7 6 5 4 3 2 1

THE American Wilderness

JOURNEYS INTO DISTANT AND HISTORIC LANDSCAPES

PHOTOGRAPHY AND TEXT BY
Stephen Gorman

FOREWORD BY
David Quammen

UNIVERSE

WILDERNESS IS A VEXED CONCEPT, as well as a rare commodity, on our planet at this end of the millennium. People of good faith and strong convictions stand in fierce disagreement, not just as to how much wilderness we should preserve, not just as to who should pay the opportunity costs of such preservation, but on a more basic question: What do we mean when we use the very word *wilderness*? Is it, as drawn from its Teutonic and Norse etymological roots, a place of wild beasts? Is it a desolate wasteland, such as the one in which Moses and his followers wandered for forty years, and in which Christ endured the temptations by Satan? Is it a pristine, verdant landscape that has remained forever uninhabited and unsullied by humanity? Is it a statutorily protected tract of land into which skiers are welcome but snowmobilers are not? Is it, in whatever form, a construct grounded upon elitist abstraction, or upon populist realism? This disagreement isn't a purely American phenomenon—there are variants around the world—but it has been especially testy in the United States within recent decades, due to our insatiable hunger for consumable landscape, and to certain facts of our freshly remembered national history.

Rich evening light ignites a cliff overlooking a remote lake in the heart of the Maine Woods. This wild territory has remained the largest uninhabited region in the lower forty-eight states.

"Wilderness was the basic ingredient of American civilization," as Roderick Nash noted in his 1967 book, *Wilderness and The American Mind.* "From the raw materials of the physical wilderness Americans built a civilization; with the idea or symbol of wilderness they sought to give that civilization identity and meaning." But in treating wilderness as a symbol, as an idea, rather than as a multifarious and richly ambivalent sort of place, we have stoked high the fire of that national disagreement.

Several years ago, almost three decades after Nash's book, the historian William Cronon published a thoughtful, provocative essay titled "The

Trouble with Wilderness," which brought some clarity to the discussion, though also additional heat. The trouble, as Cronon sees it, is that Americans have absorbed a romantic and sacralized concept of wilderness. The trouble, he argues, is that this concept (which is traceable back to the vaporous deism of Wordsworth and the faddish primitivism of Rousseau, and has been transposed to our continent largely by dreamers such as Thoreau and Muir, with the later assistance of such well-born dilettantes as Teddy Roosevelt, Owen Wister, and Bob Marshall) makes a fetish of wilderness as "virgin," uninhabited landscape. The trouble is that our idealized wilderness stands separate from humanity. The trouble is that, in its separateness, it is imputed to be somehow "truer" and more "authentically wild" than our modest town parks, our gardens, our little nature reserves, let alone our cleared, plowed, built, and settled domains. The trouble, Cronon argues, is that wilderness as thus construed represents a flight from history, a false hope of escaping responsibility for the changes that humankind has made elsewhere upon the planet. The trouble is that it embodies "a dualistic vision in which the human is entirely outside the natural." Well, jeepers, that does amount to a heap of trouble.

If the American concept of wilderness is as purblind as Cronon posits, then we have indeed wedged ourselves into a paradox. If this category of landscape is defined by its separateness from all human influence, then we can't preserve it within statutory boundaries without compromising it, can we? We can't protect it with rule-making without patronizing it. And we certainly can't visit it without breaking the sacred spell. But take heart. Fine historian and smart guy though he is, and useful as his essay may be, Bill Cronon has somewhat over-argued his case. The straw men that he knocks flat are not the sole authorities on the question. They don't reflect my concept of wilderness, they probably don't reflect yours, and they certainly don't do justice to Stephen Gorman's.

Gorman's American wilderness is not an imaginary place representing a flight from history but, on the contrary, a collection of vividly particular locales in which history itself adds to the meaning, the genius loci, and the charm. Follow his canoe down the upper Missouri River in north-central

Montana, through the Breaks, to the same Hideaway Coulee that served as refuge for Kid Curry and his pals Butch and Sundance before their last-hurrah train holdup in 1901, and you'll see what I mean. Travel with Gorman to Midway Atoll, near which Admiral Nagumo's naval strike force cruised into an ambush not long after Pearl Harbor, culminating in a sea battle that turned the momentum of World War II in the Pacific, and you'll find further evidence. Likewise with Hole-in-the-Rock Road, that improbable Mormon-cut wagon trail down into the depths of what once was Glen Canyon; likewise on the Teton Crest Traverse, among the Ten Thousand Islands, and on the rest of these forays into the American outback, wherein Gorman has shown the excellent sense to include human history, not flee from it. The common element among all the diverse and glorious landscapes celebrated here is that humanity's presence has so far fallen lightly (though not insignificantly) upon each, and that they serve therefore as salubrious reminders, not of what humans are separate from, but what in the largest context we're part of.

Back in 1967, Roderick Nash began his book with a warning: "'Wilderness' has a deceptive concreteness at first glance. The difficulty is that while the word is a noun it acts like an adjective. There is no specific material object that is wilderness." So freighted is that word with personal and symbolic meanings, he added, as to resist definition. But we've got to try. My own view is that the sensible way of defining wilderness is not in the stark dualistic terms that Cronon hears and denounces, but relativistically, as a matter of degree: Wilderness can be anyplace where human impact upon the landscape is small, reminding us therefore that we are too.

Stephen Gorman makes the same point nicely in paraphrasing one of his own heroes, the author and naturalist Sigurd Olson: "Mankind was a part of nature, he felt, interdependent with the wilderness, and he knew that human happiness and well-being rested upon strengthening our ties to the natural world." This book, with its majestic images and its companionable voice, its strenuous adventures recounted quietly, its soft steady footsteps and its smooth paddle strokes, will help strengthen exactly those ties.

—DAVID QUAMMEN, Bozeman, Montana

IN THE HIGH COUNTRY CHILL of a Wyoming morning I pulled on my scuffed boots and buckled on my worn jeans. Still half asleep, I stumbled out of the bunkhouse to the corral. Cathy, the top hand, was saddling her favorite horse, Spinnaker. At twenty-three, she was seven years my senior, and I was more than a little in awe of her. In the darkness I felt the soft, wet velvet of old Roman's nose nuzzling my hand. Stroking his bay withers, I could see the savage white streaks where a grizzly bear had laid the old mustang's back wide open.

We swam the horses across Sunlight Creek, the same stream Chief Joseph and the Nez Perce followed out of Yellowstone on their heroic flight from the U.S. Army a hundred years earlier, then climbed through the lodgepoles up to an open meadow under the rimrock. First light tinged the high Absaroka. Frost tinkled under the horses hooves, and they blew cold smoke with every breath. In the meadow we startled a bull moose, which vanished into the cover of the pines. Sometime later we watched a coyote lope home from the evening's hunt.

The herd was up Panther Creek, not far from an abandoned Indian camp we had found one day while riding after strays. Though the lodgeskins had rotted in the intervening century, the lodgepoles were still in place, and that day we rode in silent wonder among a dozen skeletal tepees. Whose lodges were they? Why were they left in place, as if the owners were fleeing some dreaded terror?

Those days on horseback were filled with magic and mystery, sweat and toil. My wages reflected my status—$100 a month plus bunk and board—but it was the best job I ever had. My real pay was spending time under open skies deep in the American outback, learning timeless skills from proud mentors, and listening to the stories they told.

A waterfall pours into a verdant chasm deep in the heart of the Maine Woods.

My boss, Doc, told me the tale of Liver-Eatin' Johnson, a mountain man who waged a personal war against the Crow. Firelight flickered over rifles and saddle blankets on the log walls, on scalp locks dangling from the wooden beams, as Doc told how Johnson—upon whose life the Robert Redford film *Jeremiah Johnson* was based—had set his traps right here in these Absaroka mountain streams. One night Fred Garlow, Buffalo Bill Cody's grandson, kept me spellbound with stories about the old days in the northern Rockies. On another occasion an elderly woman who had been born in a covered wagon told me about pioneer life on the western Nebraska frontier.

A lone skier cuts fresh tracks through a perfect blanket of fresh powder high in the northern Rockies.

Listening to these stories, I felt the power of the enduring relationships that connected the people to the land, and I experienced a deep sense of well-being, even exhilaration, as I absorbed the narratives. These stories were my stories too, I realized; they were my inheritance, and they instilled in me a powerful sense of identity and purpose.

Since then I've traveled the old trails and listened to the timeless stories in wilderness camps from Alaska to Maine. Along the way I've had the honor of working and traveling with men and women who embody the qualities that as a nation we profess to admire most: courage, self-reliance, wisdom, strength, compassion, and spiritual depth.

In my experience, the American Wilderness is the cradle of these virtues, the repository of our epic stories, and the great stage upon which we are privileged, as I have been, to reenact our national experiences. That there is a debate about the value of wilderness in America is baffling to me. We might as well debate the worth of our great libraries, galleries, museums, and universities.

Wilderness enriches us spiritually, culturally, physically, and aesthetically. It is an enduring resource that gives meaning and definition to our lives, nurtures our character, and sustains our beliefs. It is and always will be a place of magic and mystery, of sweat and toil. Here then, is a personal tribute to the American wilderness and her people.

—STEPHEN GORMAN, Exeter, New Hampshire

PADDLING
THROUGH
TIME

Allagash River Headwaters, Maine

PADDLES FLASH IN THE SUNSHINE, ripping little swirls in the surface of Maine's Caucomgomoc Lake. Five elegant wood and canvas canoes glide swiftly across the water, through a perfect mirror-image of the sky. Ahead, a loon floats upon the placid surface. He turns, looks quizzically at the canoes stealing toward him. We are, admittedly, an unusual sight. There is nothing typical of the late twentieth century about our little flotilla—we are travelers from another era.

The loon watches a moment longer, then tilts his head back and laughs. It is the haunting laugh of a lunatic. Behind us, another loon answers, then another. Soon, the lake is ringing with the maniacal laughter of loons.

Beyond a line of green hills to the west, a forest stretches unbroken to the border with Quebec. Far to the south, across a watery maze of streams, bogs, and woods, is Moosehead Lake and the last town, Greenville, the traditional starting point for journeys into the Maine Woods. To the east, hidden beyond the horizon, rise the mile-high ramparts of Katahdin in Baxter State Park. And to the north, in the direction we are heading, the Maine Woods reach deep into the belly of Canada.

We are paddling the headwater lakes of the Allagash River, heart of Maine's fabled canoe country. At over ten million acres, the Maine Woods encompass a region some five times the size of Yellowstone National Park. And in all that area there isn't a single paved road. Largely owned by private timber companies, these woods and waters are the largest uninhabited region in the lower forty-eight states. Swinging my paddle, gazing down the lake at miles of undisturbed shoreline, Henry David Thoreau's words come to mind: "What a place to live," he said, "what a place to die and be buried in!"

Thoreau passed through here twice in the mid-1800s. Unskilled in the ways of the wilderness, Thoreau hired experienced woodsmen to lead him

An elegant handmade wood and canvas canoe glides across a lake in Maine.

through the forest. His guide on the 1853 trip was Joe Aitteon, and on the 1857 journey, Joe Polis. Both men were Penobscots from Indian Island near Old Town, Maine. Thoreau later crafted his journals from those trips into the book he called *The Maine Woods*.

The current view from a canoe is remarkably unchanged since Thoreau's day, and to find your way here it is still advisable to hire the right guides. Were Henry here with us, I suspect he would cast an appraising glance at our guides and tersely nod his approval.

In the canoe next to mine, Maine Guide Alexandra Conover is paddling solo, her yellow hand-carved paddle knifing through the water with effortless grace. She paddles like a Penobscot, using short strokes, slicing the blade back underwater on the recovery.

Alexandra is a slender young woman, lean and hard, with auburn tresses spilling down to her shoulders from under a broad-brimmed hat. Wearing the traditional garb of the Maine guide—red-checked shirt, beige khakis, and dark-tanned L.L. Bean boots—she powers the loaded boat while keeping up a cheerful banter. Despite her slim frame, I know she can toss that canoe on her shoulders and trot down a portage trail as quickly as an unsuspecting client can offer to lend a hand.

Garrett Conover, also a Maine Guide, is in the stern of the canoe ahead. He has a full dark beard and wears steel-rimmed glasses. A head taller than his wife, dressed in a similar outfit, he too has the lean hard muscles that come from paddling, poling, and portaging loaded canoes along wilderness waterways day after day, year after year.

When Garrett and Alexandra Conover go off to the Maine Woods, they leave the triumphs of late twentieth-century camping technology behind. Instead of modern, freeze-dried camp fare, they bring whole foods and bake bread daily in a reflector oven set close by a fire. They pack food and equipment in handmade wanigan boxes and pack baskets. They make leather tumplines to carry gear and canoes over portage trails. They carve their paddles and setting poles using the old-time woodsman's favorite tool, the crooked knife—a single-handed draw knife found in bush camps throughout the north.

In the canoe next to mine, Maine Guide Alexandra Conover paddles solo, her yellow hand-carved paddle knifing through the water with effortless grace.

Having spent the last twenty years studying the traditional wilderness skills refined by generations of Indians and guides, the Conovers have no peers among the contemporary guides registered by the state of Maine. Their unique service, North Woods Ways, is dedicated to the efficient and reliable methods developed by woodland travelers of earlier eras. Despite their relative youth—they are both in their early forties—they are practically living legends. Mention their names anywhere in canoe country—from Maine to Minnesota, from Labrador to Manitoba—and chances are good that experienced woodsmen will know of them.

Of course, the Conovers would scoff at such notions. Last night by the campfire Garrett expressed his modest desire to "someday move through the wilderness and across the seasons with as much skill as any four-year-old native kid."

There is an enduring mystique associated with the Maine Guide. He, and today she, is a direct descendent of the oldest American mythic figures—Leatherstocking, Daniel Boone, and a hundred other American archetypes. The Maine Guide must be expert at canoe and camp craft, first aid, route finding, and other wilderness skills. He must pass a written test, then convince a board of examiners of his qualifications in an oral exami-

OVERLEAF:
The mile-high ramparts of Mount Katahdin rise above the West Branch of the Penobscot River.

A madcap choir of coyotes serenaded us as the light left the northern sky and we returned to our camp beneath a tall stand of white pine, cedar, and fragrant balsam fir.

nation. If the board senses a weakness in her knowledge or skills, they probe the sensitive spot until they are certain she will bring her clients back safely. If any doubt remains, they will fail her on the spot.

So far we have enjoyed sun-soaked days and star-swept nights. Last night, after the dinner dishes were put back in the wanigan (an Algonquian word for the wooden box we use for storing camp wares), we skimmed for miles across Loon Lake in empty canoes as the setting sun turned the black waters to liquid gold. A madcap choir of coyotes serenaded us as the light left the northern sky and we returned to our camp beneath a tall stand of white pine, cedar, and fragrant balsam fir.

There are nine of us, counting our guides and their fifteen-year-old junior apprentice, Jeff DePasquale. We are exploring streams, lakes, and ponds far off the usual canoe routes. We are poking around in no great hurry, watching for moose, letting the woods and waters work their magic on us.

There comes a moment on a canoe trip when you cross a threshold and realize you could keep going like this forever. The feeling generally sets in on the second or third day, when your creaky muscles loosen, when eight or nine hours of deep slumber under the forest canopy restores you, and when temporal cares assume their proper size and fade into insignificance.

Here, on Caucomgomoc Lake heading toward Ciss Stream, we have crossed that threshold. Looking around at the other canoes, I see friends who were strangers forty-eight hours ago. Ahead, Judy and Ned Garner are gliding along in their newly restored 1916 E. M. White wood and canvas guide canoe. For them, this trip is the fulfillment of a dream. Close by are

Barbara and Reed Anthony; they have traveled with the Conovers before, as has my canoeing partner, Glen Takata, who is on his ninth or tenth trip with Garrett and Alexandra.

We are an eclectic congregation, including a Ph.D. in ethnomusicology, two university administrators, a chief financial officer, a computer software designer, and a hard-bitten journalist. With so many backgrounds and interests represented, our talk has been lively and enriching. We have retold epic tales of northern exploration, quoted Thoreau, discussed classic canoe trips in the Canadian North. Everyone brings something different to the campfire, but we all have one thing in common—a love of wilderness and a desire to learn the Conovers' special style of canoe tripping.

The Conovers' style runs counter to the contemporary grain. Eschewing synthetics, Garrett and Alexandra wear neither Gore-Tex—"Leak-Tex," as Garrett calls the self-proclaimed "miracle fiber"—nor polyester pile, both mainstays of the modern camper's wardrobe. Instead, they choose comfortable natural fibers such as cotton and wool. Absent from their fleet are the aluminum and plastic canoes of the major manufacturers. Instead, the Conovers use finely handcrafted wood and canvas canoes of a design used by Maine Guides over a century ago. With their gleaming varnished ribs, their sharp entry and exit lines, and their lively, responsive feel, these canoes are a joy to travel in. And they are tougher than they look, requiring only a little more awareness of sharp rocks and shallows than a modern canoe. But if we *did* break a rib, thwart, or gunwale, either Conover would carve a replacement from natural materials close at hand. The traveler with a wrecked synthetic canoe, on the other hand, would find himself afoot and possibly in serious trouble.

The Conovers' adherence to the old ways is neither a romantic attempt to bring back an earlier era, nor a desire to role-play in some sort of mobile living-history exhibit.

"We're not old-timey for old-time's sake," says a grinning Garrett, who encourages questions regarding their methods. "Natives and guides developed these skills ten thousand years ago, and they're as useful as ever. The

Everyone brings something different to the campfire, but we all have something in common—a love of wilderness and a desire to learn the ways of the wild that still work best.

tools are functional, durable, and easily repaired. Put it this way: these methods have yet to be replaced."

Rather than a lesson in antiquity, what we seek from the Conovers is an alternative to what Garrett calls "the prepackaged, consumer-culture outdoor experience." What they offer their clients, he says, is "a viable alternative to the technology that provides a dangerous substitute for critical wilderness skills and that prevents people from developing an awareness of the environment they are traveling through." That's why we're here: to learn the ways of the wilderness that still work best.

The Conovers are studious about their traditional craft, but they are hardly severe schoolmasters, and the boat-to-boat conversations are filled with jokes and laughter. Garrett has a fine sense for the absurd, keeping us in stitches with his droll comments and wordplay, while Alexandra could easily take the stage as a professional *raconteur*. Her accents, gestures, and facial expressions bring a dozen north woods characters to life.

The Conovers' style runs counter to the contemporary grain; they use finely handcrafted canoes of a design perfected by Maine Guides over a century ago.

We enter Ciss Stream, a meandering deadwater with no perceptible current, and our voices drop to a whisper. This is textbook moose country. Quietly we paddle past the limbs, trunks, and toppled root structures of ghostly dead trees lining both sides of the grassy meadow. The lifeless silver forms reach skyward, creating a spooky and entrancing scene. Called "dry-ki" (the words rhyme) by the loggers, a term short for "dry-killed," the trees were drowned when driving dams were built on Caucomgomoc over a century ago.

We have already seen three or four moose today and an equal number the day before, so we enter Ciss Stream full of anticipation. We aren't disappointed. Around the first bend we encounter a young bull feeding on lilies, reeds, and eel grass. He keeps chewing as he dully contemplates our intrusion, then lumbers off on his spindly legs through the meadow. Long after he disappears from sight we follow his progress by the enormous racket he makes smashing through the woods.

"Stealthy, isn't he?" Alexandra says with a grin.

Thoreau thought the moose a homely creature. "The moose is singularly grotesque and awkward to look at," he complained. "Why should it stand so high at the shoulders? Why have so long a head? Why have no tail to speak of? . . . They made me think of great frightened rabbits, with their long ears and half-inquisitive, half-frightened looks. . . ."

Around the next bend the scene is repeated, this time a magnificent bull with a full, broad rack. And on each of the next several bends we

A canoeist portages around the thunderous cataract of Allagash Falls.

encounter moose—young bulls, cows, cows with fuzzy little calves. By now our conversation has picked up again, we spend less time watching. We are becoming jaded, the novelty of moose wearing off.

"I'd like to see the next moose do something different, like a cartwheel or something," says young Jeff. No such luck. Around the next bend we come face-to-face with another cow chomping placidly in midstream.

"Why won't they leave us alone!" cries Glen in a mock plaintive voice.

Our camp on Daggett Pond is exquisite. Upon our arrival, a bald eagle flaps away on great wing beats. Thick coniferous forest rings the pond, a rough circle a mile in diameter. A half dozen loons are out on the lake, the rippling V of their wakes reflecting in the late afternoon light. The birds chuckle among themselves, as if sharing a private joke. To the northwest we can see the rocky ridgeline that rises to the summit of Allagash Mountain.

Tonight, a steady rain slashes down through the tall pines. But before we have a chance to grab our raingear, Garrett rigs a spacious canopy of a rainfly, raising it high above our heads with the eleven-foot-long setting poles carried in each canoe. The result is a shelter we can stand under without hunching over, that keeps us dry, and that protects the fire from the rain. Though the drops are drumming heavily, the change in the weather causes no inconvenience, and we enjoy another of Alexandra's distinctive meals. Tonight's menu is chicken stir-fry, topped off with a blueberry pie that she whipped together and baked in the reflector oven while we chatted.

The rain slows, then stops. Rich beams of orange light illuminate the far shore. Garrett wonders aloud whether to take down the tarp. "If I do," he moans, "it'll probably rain for a month!"

Over dinner, Alexandra tells us how she chose the life of a Maine Guide. Raised in the Boston suburb of Stow, she is the daughter of parents who urged her to follow her heart. At an early age she discovered the books of Ernest Thompson Seton, the nineteenth-century naturalist who wrote lyrically about the far north. From that time on, her path was set. "Those books put a wrinkle in the course of my life," she says.

When she was eight years old, her teacher asked her to draw a picture of what she would do if she had a million dollars. "I drew myself sitting next to a birch-bark canoe pulled up on a beach," she says with a grin.

Garrett, too, dreamed of a wilderness life while growing up in the Berkshire Hills of western Massachusetts, though at first he was drawn to the Rocky Mountain West. But after a period studying wildlife biology and creative writing at the University of Montana, he transferred to the College of the Atlantic, in Bar Harbor, Maine, where Alexandra Brown was matriculating.

It seems inevitable that they should have met and that they should have found their mentor, Mick Fahey, the man who would exert the most profound influence upon their lives. In the fall of 1976, Alexandra heard that one of the last of the old-time Maine Guides was retired and living near Bar Harbor. One day she looked him up and introduced herself. The two became fast friends—she wanted a teacher, he wanted to pass on his knowledge.

"Mick was my university," she says now.

Mick's father had been boss of the Penobscot River log drive, and each spring and summer young Fahey, whose real name was Francis, would go off with his father's crew to learn the ways of the woods. The river drivers, mostly Penobscots, took him under their wing. They affectionately called

Henry David Thoreau thought the moose a homely creature. "The moose is singularly awkward to look at," he complained. "Why should it stand so high at the shoulders? Why have so long a head? Why have no tail to speak of?"

him "Mickey" and taught him to handle a canoe, axe, peavey, and pick pole. They brought him deep into the forest, showed him how to hunt and trap, to make snowshoes and pack baskets, to build bark canoes. In 1923, at the age of seventeen, Fahey became the youngest registered guide in Maine.

In the late seventies, Mick and his wife, Eunice, decided to retire to Chesuncook Village, a tiny settlement in the heart of the Maine Woods without phones, electricity, or roads to the outside world. When they did, Alexandra and Garrett went along as apprentices. In Chesuncook, Mick taught them to use the crooked knife, to make moccasins, to paddle a canoe with the efficient north woods stroke, and to pole one up shallow rapids.

In 1980, Garrett and Alexandra married, passed their guide's test, and started North Woods Ways—all of which brought a sense of fulfillment to the old guide, who passed away in 1984.

Morning brings clear skies, and Garrett, Ned, and I hike the three-mile trail to Allagash Mountain. In the dripping woods the air is perfumed with the scent of wild strawberries. Deer and moose tracks wander aimlessly across the muddy path. We pass two beaver dams and watch in amusement as dozens of tiny toads the size of pencil erasers hop across the trail. We examine a tree trunk that a bear has clawed apart to get at the insects inside the rotting wood.

Atop Allagash Mountain we find a fire tower unlocked and unoccupied. With clear skies and little humidity, the view is stunning. I recall Thoreau's words from the top of Katahdin, which is clearly visible far to the southeast: "It did not look as if a solitary traveler had cut so much as a walking stick there."

Close inspection through binoculars, however, tells quite a different story, for in the distance we can see expansive clear-cuts rolling off to the horizon. With impressive precision and clinical efficiency, the loggers have left nothing standing. This naturally brings Thoreau to mind again. He protested that the loggers had no more right to take all the trees than "individual speculators were to be allowed to export the clouds out of the sky, or the stars out of the firmament, one by one."

We look in all directions and, except for the cutting, see no other sign of humanity. Allagash Lake at the foot of the mountain is miles long, dotted with emerald islands, and rimmed here and there with gleaming granite outcrops. We see moose and deer wading in shallow bays and feeder streams far below.

The current view from a canoe is remarkably unchanged since Thoreau's day. Were Henry here with us, I suspect he would cast an appraising glance at our guides and tersely nod his approval.

We break camp on our final day, once again under bright blue skies. By afternoon we have come full circle—almost. All that remains is a two-mile section of shallow white water that must be negotiated—upstream. Out come the spruce setting poles, and after a brief lesson in their use, we head for the churning, boulder-studded tongue of water pouring down from the lake above.

To my amazement, it works. Instead of carrying canoes and gear through the tangled blowdowns along the bank—a project that would take hours—we use the poles to hop from eddy to eddy, shoving the boats up the glassy chutes between rocks. In less time than it would take to walk, we ascend the frolicsome river. Too soon it seems, for this is great fun, we reach the head of the rapid, and the van comes into view. The trip is over.

Not quite. The moose still won't leave us alone, and on the long drive back through the woods we encounter the gawky creatures standing by the side of the logging road, crossing ahead of us, racing alongside us.

"How many is that?" asks Barbara.

"Thirty-six, by my count," answers Judy.

"Let's go for forty!" says young Jeff, pressing his nose to the dusty window.

—

WATER
AND
SKY

Everglades National Park, Florida

THE STORM THAT CHURNED the Gulf Coast waters into café au lait has finally blown itself out, leaving a bright, sparkling day in its wake. Halfway through a ten-day Everglades canoe journey, Dan Berns and I welcome the reprieve from fighting big waves, headwinds, and cold lashing rain.

Now, resisting the urge to bask in the warm south Florida sunshine, I tug on the broad brim of my hat and roll down my shirtsleeves to guard against the intense subtropical rays. I take a stroke, then another. The canoe slips forward, gains momentum. As I glide across the glassy waters, I peer over the gunwale to sound the ocean depths.

A mile off the coast of Lostmans Key in the Gulf of Mexico, deep in the heart of the Ten Thousand Islands, way out on the wild edge of Everglades National Park, the distance to the bottom is measured not in fathoms, but in inches. Looking through the flashing surface with my polarized sunglasses, an absolute necessity here, I see there's a good two feet of water beneath the hull.

Suspended between earth and sky, I'm captivated by the sight of blue crabs scuttling along the ocean floor. Turtle grass sways languidly in the gentle current. Big fish—sheepshead, sea trout, redfish—dart ahead of the canoe, pushing up big bulges of water as they streak across the shallows. Not so easily spooked, a tarpon hangs motionless in the water like a hundred-pound, armor-plated submarine. Drifting in and out of view like a phantom, a sawfish waves his lethal snout back and forth, no doubt hunting a school of mullet. Further on, a stingray flies gracefully past on undulating wings, searching for mollusks and crustaceans to crunch in its powerful jaws. Sometime later I watch the triangular dorsal fin of a blacktip shark shear the water not twenty feet off the starboard bow.

The enormous Everglades sky dwarfs a lone canoeist off Rabbit Key in the Ten Thousand Islands.

On the western edge of Everglades National Park, water and sky merge into one. This is one of the most mysterious and bewitching places I've ever seen.

The bottom drops off. I pass over a channel cut by the ebb and flow of Lostmans River, a brackish, alligator-filled estuarine passage slicing through the thin green swath of mangrove islands marking the eastern horizon. Suddenly, the water all around my canoe explodes in huge boils and violent upwellings that rock the boat back and forth as gouts of water burst in the air. I reach out and slap my paddle flat against the water in a low brace to keep from capsizing. As I do, I can just make out the enormous dark shapes of a half-dozen West Indian manatees, who are probably every bit as startled as I am.

Heart pounding, adrenaline rushing, I head to shore, slog the last thirty yards across the sienna mudflats and razor-sharp oyster beds, and relax on the beach against a desiccated driftwood log. Still keyed up from

my encounter with the thousand-pound manatees, I focus on a cloud of white ibis settling onto an emerging sandbar. The birds probe the flats with scythe-shaped bills for shrimp and crabs. Great blue herons stalk the shallows with the infinite patience of true hunters. A squadron of brown pelicans dive-bombs the water, smacking the slick surface and gulping hapless mullet. From time to time the mullet leap clear of the water in frantic attempts to get away and get on with their own feeding.

My breathing has barely returned to normal when I hear something large smashing through the hardwood hammock directly behind me. Alarmed, I turn toward the sound as a feral hog bursts through the ferns, vines, and gumbo limbo trees onto the beach a few yards away. I expect him to flee when he sees me, but instead he raises his snout, catches my scent, and takes a few quick steps in my direction.

Eyeing his sharp tusks, impressed by his clear intent to possess the beach, I back off until I reach my canoe and paddle away to rejoin Dan, who detoured to fish near the mouth of Lostmans River. Satisfied that I've abandoned the beach, the hog turns to root through the brush. Oblivious to both the pig's presence and mine, a white-tailed deer emerges from the dense vegetation and walks slowly down the beach. Above us all, a bald

Dan Berns paddles his canoe through rough seas in the Gulf of Mexico off Lostmans Key.

eagle circles on broad black wings. Riding a thermal lift in a wide and graceful spiral, he climbs higher and higher in the pale blue arch of sky.

Traveling slowly and quietly under my own power, totally immersed in this watery environment as only a canoeist or kayaker can be, I'm learning that everything in the Ten Thousand Islands is part of the food chain— including, I remind myself, the occasional unwary paddler. But that's the hallmark of an intact, functioning environment and a true wilderness, and I wouldn't be here otherwise.

A world away from the banalities of Orlando, the throbbing, high-voltage enticements of Miami Beach, and the sprawling suburbs of Tampa, the Ten Thousand Islands are one of this country's last great wildernesses, a place almost no one knows and even fewer visit. Situated far from any road, the islands are a lost labyrinth of mangroves, hardwood hammocks, and dark, brackish rivers flowing to the white sandy shores of the Gulf of Mexico.

Fringing the southwest coast of Florida from Marco Island to Cape Sable, the Ten Thousand Islands are home to some of the world's most extensive mangrove swamps, a vital transition zone where fresh water seeping from the Everglades mingles with the salt water of the sea. The result is an almost unimaginable profusion of marine, terrestrial, and avian life. And the mangroves themselves, sometimes called "walking trees" because of their stilt-like root structures, are a key to this incredible fecundity.

For all their visual monotony, the mangroves provide numerous benefits to the prolific life of the tide-flooded coastal swamps. Rising from the mud deposits overlying the limestone substrate that forms the Florida

peninsula, the nearly impenetrable mangrove roots offer important nursing grounds and critical sanctuary for numerous species of fish and crustaceans, including many that are commercially valuable as adults. West Indies spiny lobsters, for example, spend their first two years of life in the shelter of the mangrove roots. Above the tide line, the mangrove's upper branches provide important roosting and nesting sites for the astonishing wealth of bird life found here: herons, egrets, white ibis, brown pelicans, and frigate birds, among many others. The entire archipelago forms a many-miles-wide protective barrier for the otherwise exposed interior environments, blunting the devastating effects of violent hurricanes, tropical storms, and floods.

Although the Ten Thousand Islands are now uninhabited, they weren't always so. The region's first human occupants were the Calusa, who took up residence some two thousand years ago. Remarkably, the Calusa actually built much of the high ground required for human habitation in the islands. Their shell mounds, literally the result of centuries of oyster shucking, remain above sea level even in hurricanes. Some of these mounds are enormous. Chokoloskee Mound, where Dan and I began our trip and where the Calusa are credited with slaying Spanish explorer Ponce de Leon in 1521, spans some 130 acres and reaches a height of twenty feet in places. You can still see the shells as you paddle by places where the current has exposed clean cross sections to view.

The Calusa, who numbered perhaps 20,000 at time of first contact, died out in the mid-1700s, the victims of Spanish conquest, the slave trade, and European diseases for which they possessed no immunity. They were replaced by Indians of various tribes fleeing white encroachment in Alabama, Georgia, and South Carolina. Banding together, these Indians called themselves Seminoles, from the Creek Indian word *semoli*, meaning "runaways." Harried by the U.S. Army during the mid-nineteenth century, the Seminoles took refuge here in the backwater rivers and islands. An estimated 200 Seminoles survived the Army's last attempt to wipe them out in 1858; their descendants live in small Everglades communities to this day.

The Seminoles weren't the only people to hide out in the Ten Thousand Islands. Escaped slaves, convicts, outlaws, hermits, and other odd and eccentric characters found refuge here. Edgar J. Watson, rumored to have been an outlaw and murderer out West, showed up in the islands in 1892. He farmed sugarcane and vegetables on an old Calusa shell mound along the Chatham River, shipping his produce to market in Key West and Tampa.

Watson prospered in the islands, in part because he saved on labor costs by killing his hired hands. In 1910, after committing a triple murder at Lostmans Key, Watson was gunned down by vigilantes on the dock at Chokoloskee. According to some sources, more than fifty graves were later discovered on his property, now a National Park Service backcountry campsite.

Plume hunters and gator poachers moved into the area in the late nineteenth and early twentieth centuries, and the wildlife suffered grievously. But the havoc caused by a few individuals pales when compared to the destruction wrought by more than a half century of unbridled growth and development, growth that shows no sign of slowing. Politically powerful agricultural and development interests have disrupted and polluted the historic flow of life-giving water to the Everglades with an extensive system of canals and levees. The number of wading birds nesting in the southern Everglades, for example, has declined 93 percent, from 265,000 in the 1930s to just 18,500 today.

The outlook for the "River of Grass," as conservationist Marjorie Stoneman Douglas described the sheet of water seeping across south Florida from Lake Okeechobee to Florida Bay, remains grim. But it's not just special interests that are to blame: Florida's human population grows by nearly 1,000 people daily. An additional 200,000 gallons of water must be diverted for human use every twenty-four hours.

The Ten Thousand Islands are home to some of the world's most extensive mangrove swamps. The mangroves are sometimes called "walking trees" because of their stilt-like root structure.

In efforts to stave off disaster, Congress has made some funding available to acquire critical parcels of neighboring land, to restore wetlands, and to reroute the vast web of diversion canals in order to ensure a more natural flow of water to the Everglades. But the magnitude of the problem is daunting, and the price tag for restoration is currently projected to reach $5 billion. However, the Everglades are simply too precious to lose.

In camp at Highland Beach just south of Lostmans River, Dan and I set up the tent and put the dinner pot on the stove to simmer. Here in the Ten Thousand Islands, the battle over the Everglades seems mercifully distant. Relaxing on this long lonely strand out on the far edge of the world, I've succeeded in putting it all behind me, if only for a while. Now, it's time to enjoy being here in the islands, to study the bands of pastel evening colors washed across the enormous sky. It occurs to me that after five days, there are still parts of this sky I haven't seen. I make a mental note to pay

Relaxing on this long lonely strand at the edge of the world, I've succeeded in literally putting it all behind me. Now it's time to study the bands of pastel evening colors washed across the enormous sky.

more attention.

The Everglades may be in trouble, but this is still one of the most mysterious and bewitching places I've ever been. Watching the big red sun sink into the Gulf, I remember paddling among a family of bottlenose dolphins slashing like thunderbolts through a school of mullet off Rabbit Key. Four or five of them broke off from the pack and swam alongside my canoe for a hundred yards or so, close enough to touch, rolling over time and again to look me in the eye.

A warm breeze rustling the palm fronds behind me brings me back to the present, and I watch a large shark cruise past the beach not ten yards from where I'm perched on the sand in my camp chair, writing these words in my journal.

As if I could ever forget.

VOYAGEUR
COUNTRY

Boundary Waters Canoe Area Wilderness, Minnesota

WE THREADED THE CANOES through the eye of a narrow inlet, past the rocky points guarding the entrance to the deeply recessed cove, and emerged onto an expansive lake stretching off into the hazy blue distance. An open horizon, broken here and there by low-lying islands and evergreen peninsulas, lay before us.

Suddenly, navigation was no longer a simple matter of following the familiar shoreline. The lake was a maze of options, a hundred different ways we could go, each with its own enticements. I stopped paddling and drifted for a moment, scanned the shore, then oriented the map, making the rugged features of the landscape conform to the squiggly lines drawn on the flat sheet of paper. I took out my compass, chose a bearing, and aligned it with the "direction of travel" arrow on the base plate. I knew it would take time to get used to the scale of things, to make the translation between the actual world and its two-dimensional representation. Until then we would tick off every rocky point, every island we passed, until we felt at home in the landscape.

For mile after mile we ascend the twisting stream. The country is wild, the portages little-used, and we see no other people.

We were in the Boundary Waters Canoe Area Wilderness in northern Minnesota, a rugged region of forests, rivers, exposed bedrock ridges, and countless lakes. Over a million acres in size and stretching for nearly 200 miles along the Canadian border, the Boundary Waters contains some 1,200 miles of canoe routes. Indeed, nearly half of my map was colored in blue.

Somewhere along the southern shore, about three miles distant, the portage trail began at the bottom of a small, featureless bay. Only a foot or two wide and concealed by thick trees, the trail was as invisible as a thread laid across a living room carpet. Yet in all that vast open space, we had to find that one path. We also needed to limber up muscles still stiff from days of car travel, adjust to the pace of human-powered motion, and let the worries and stress of modern life yield to the healing power of the wilderness.

The great naturalist, wilderness guide, and author Sigurd Olson spent a lifetime exploring the canoe routes of the Boundary Waters. Unfailingly appreciative of both the rigors and the beauty of wild places, Olson was a tireless advocate of wilderness preservation, and it is largely due to his efforts that this and many other large tracts of open space throughout the United States were saved from development. Mankind was a part of nature, he felt, interdependent with the wilderness, and he knew that human happiness and well-being rested upon strengthening our ties to the natural world. Olson experienced a profound sense of peace and harmony in wilderness that he could never find in cities and towns.

"This way of existence, living in tents and traveling together each day, seemed the way life should be," he wrote in *The Lonely Land*, a gripping chronicle of a 500-mile canoe journey through the Canadian North. "There are few places left on the North American continent where men can still see the country as it was before Europeans came and know some of the challenges and freedoms of those who saw it first." Thanks to Olson, the Boundary Waters is still one of those places, and as the lake unfolded before us I said a silent word of appreciation to the old *bourgeois*, or leader, as Olson's closest friends called him.

Sometime later we guided our canoes past a rocky islet shaped like a

As the stifling afternoon wears on, we search for the outlet of a narrow stream. We find it at the bottom of a shallow bay. The little river slithers like a snake across a broad valley between parallel ridges.

fishhook. Just beyond it, the shoreline fell away sharply to the south, exactly as the map indicated it should. A knob of rock stuck out into open water, and then the bay opened up to the left. Squinting through the midday August glare, I could just make out a slight opening in the cedars at the end of the bay, our portage trail, the first of many. As always at the beginning of a trip, I took some satisfaction in finding my way across miles of complicated terrain to a specific spot on the map.

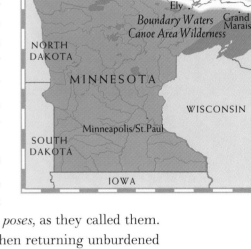

Careful not to scrape the loaded canoes against the sharp rocks lying just beneath the surface, my wife, Mary, and I stepped out of the boats into the shallows and lifted out the packs, put them ashore, then returned for the canoes. According to the map, the portage was more than a mile and a half across, traversing several rocky ridges, and skirting a series of beaver ponds connected by a meandering stream—a rugged carry, but one we hoped would put us into a little-traveled part of the wilderness.

With two canoes and four packs there was no way we could cross the portage in one trip. Instead, we decided to adopt the strategy of the French Canadian *voyageurs* and do the carry in stages, or *poses,* as they called them. By portaging half the load to the midway point, then returning unburdened for the second half, we planned to leap-frog the gear forward, taking advantage of frequent rest breaks. Either way we did it, the carry required three full crossings—a hike of four and a half miles—but the *posé* method meant lighter loads and less chance of fatigue-related stress or even injury as we adapted to the rigors of Boundary Waters canoe tripping.

The portage, like most in the Boundary Waters, was probably first used by Sioux Indians hundreds of years ago. Prior to the 1700s, the Sioux, who for many represent the apotheosis of Plains Indian horse culture, were still a forest people living in the Upper Great Lakes region. In the seventeenth and early eighteenth centuries the Sioux migrated out onto the Great Plains, an exodus hastened by their enemies, the Ojibwa, a word sometimes corrupted into "Chippewa" by early explorers. Armed with European guns obtained in trade, the Ojibwa established themselves as masters of the lake country.

The Ojibwa were one of the largest Indian groups on the continent, numbering an estimated 35,000, and their enormous territory stretched from the shores of Lake Huron west across Lake Superior and Minnesota all the way to Turtle Mountain in North Dakota, and from Lake Winnipeg and James Bay south to Wisconsin and Michigan. To travel through this watery domain required specific skills, and the Ojibwa were master builders and paddlers of birch-bark canoes. Similar to the Sioux on the plains, the Ojibwa also came to represent the apex of a culture, though theirs was built upon canoes and canoe travel.

I hoisted the heavy green canvas Duluth pack, then tossed my canoe onto my shoulders and took off down the trail at a quick trot. Over the years I've learned that it isn't just the distance across a portage that sets your muscles to screaming, it's the amount of time the weight rests on your shoulders. The quicker across, the less pain. Soon my feet were shuffling rapidly forward as I dodged rocks, skirted muddy streams, and clambered over an occasional fallen tree. Mary was right behind with her own canoe and one of the red waterproof gear bags.

Climbing a sharp rocky bluff, we reached the height of land and estimated we were halfway across. Gratefully we eased the canoes onto the matted caribou moss, lay the packs down, and savored the relaxing walk back for the second load through the cool birch and pine forest.

The undisputed masters at portaging were the voyageurs, the canoemen who paddled the continent's far-flung network of waterways in the service of the Hudson Bay and Northwest Companies. During the heyday of the fur trade, roughly 1650 to 1850, they paddled from ice-out in the spring to freeze-up in the fall, sometimes covering thousands of miles over the course of a season.

Dressed in bright red caps, colorful, billowy shirts with braided sashes, and deerskin leggings and moccasins, the voyageurs were a picturesque company of adventurers. With their brightly painted paddles flashing, they departed Montreal in *canots de maître*—thirty-six-foot-long birch-bark canoes paddled by up to fifteen men. These huge freighters hauled four tons of cargo, every pound of which was carried over dozens of portages on the men's backs. The canoes traveled in a long and colorful line—up to thirty canoes per brigade. As they embarked from Lachine, a few miles from Montreal, the brigades were blessed by a priest, then each canoe was sent off to the hinterlands with an eight-gallon keg of brandy.

The first night out, the voyageurs drained their kegs, then, fiercely hung over, they worked their way up the Ottawa River and then the Mattawa, crossed the height of land, and floated down the French River to Georgian Bay on Lake Huron. Traveling westward, they coasted the rugged and stormy north shore of Lake Superior. They were often under way by four in the morning, singing the *chansons* of the Loire Valley as the miles slid under the keel. Every hour they stopped to rest and smoke their pipes. For the voyageurs, distances were measured not in miles, but in *pipes*. After sixteen or eighteen hours on the water, paddling some fifty miles, they made camp for the night, sleeping like dead men under the overturned canoes.

They were small of stature, these farm boys from the valley of the St. Lawrence River, rarely over five feet five—larger men took up too much precious cargo space in the canoes. But they were strong, and on the many portages each voyageur was responsible for six packs, or *pièces*. Filled with blankets, pins, beads, guns and ammunition, calico, and kegs of rum, trade

We were in a rugged region of forests, rivers, exposed bedrock ridges, and countless lakes. An open horizon, broken here and there by low-lying islands and evergreen peninsulas, lies before us.

—

goods for the tribes of the interior, the packs weighed ninety pounds apiece, and rarely did a voyageur set off across a portage with fewer than two packs on his back, one stacked atop the other.

Thus burdened with 180 pounds each, they ran the portages. Not only was running ultimately the best strategy, voyageur pride required it— portages were a chance to show off. One voyageur managed to astonish even his fellows when he set out carrying seven *pièces*, a load of some 630 pounds. Hernia was not an infrequent cause of death among the voyageurs. Others drowned in rapids when their canoes overturned—few could swim a stroke. As many as thirty wooden crosses lined the banks above particularly dangerous falls.

As tough as their lives were, the voyageurs were tougher, and they loved what they did. Said one voyageur in old age, "I could carry, paddle, walk, and sing with any man I ever saw. I have been twenty-four years a canoe man . . . no portage was ever too long for me. Fifty songs could I sing. I have saved the lives of ten voyageurs. Have had twelve wives and six running dogs. I spent all my money in pleasure. Were I young again, I should spend my life the same way over. There is no life so happy as a voyageur's life!"

Two days and many portages later, Mary and I cross another height of land. Through the trees we see the welcome sparkle of sunlight on water at trail's end, always a thrilling sight on any carry. The lake is perhaps a mile long and a half-mile wide, rimmed with polished gray rock reaching to a height of thirty feet above the mirror surface. At the far end of the lake I can just see the beginning of the next portage, but there's no question of moving on. It's been a grueling day, worthy of the voyageurs, and this lake makes us an offer of rest we can't refuse. The sun is hovering above the line of ragged spruce to the west, and it's time to make camp. We stroke the canoes straight as arrows toward the high dome of rock and are delighted to see that the summit is open and flat, a perfect spot, with a fine view up and down the lake. Nearby, at the base of the ledge, we find a gently sloping shelf of rock reaching gradually into the water. We step out of the canoes, the cool water grips our legs, and we unload the gear onto the shore.

The tent goes up in a sheltered nook behind a screen of balsam fir. We place the kitchen up on top of the open dome. Behind camp, back in the woods, we locate a tall birch with a sturdy branch protruding about twenty feet off the ground, perfect for hanging food out of the reach of the many black bears that haunt these woods and waters. In the iridescent glow of

The lake's shallows reflect a mirror image of the evening sky.

OVERLEAF:
The summit of the high dome of rock is open and flat, a perfect campsite with a commanding view up and down the lake.

sunset we have a hot fire crackling, the dinner pots are on, and from our resting place high above the water, we're toasting the silence, the solitude, and the shadowy but palpable presence of the voyageurs.

The loons wake us. The lake echoes with their haunting laughter, and we exit the tent at first light. On the lake a half-dozen of the birds are calling to each other across the water, and their wails are answered by loons on other unseen lakes nearby. We hear the whistling of wings overhead, and sleek black-and-white loons fly past on five-foot wings, circle the lake, then land on their bellies, sledding across the water and raising wakes for ten or fifteen yards until they skid to a halt. More loons fly in, a half-dozen or more, some flying beneath us as we watch from the rocky heights.

The birds cruise the lake with their eyes just beneath the surface. Trolling for fish, every now and then one dives into the black water and disappears. We try to guess where he will reappear, but we're always wrong. Every now and then one looks up from the water, leans back and flaps his wings, and utters a weird, ghostly tremolo. All the loons on the lake pick up the refrain until the air fills with their confused but wild and thrilling medley, a primeval, unearthly sound that gives voice to the spirit of the northern wilderness.

And then I hear a jarring, discordant note. The metal clang of an aluminum canoe being dropped on the rocks at the end of the portage trail breaks the spell and jostles us rudely back into the present.

The undisputed masters at portaging were the voyageurs, the canoemen who paddled the continent's far-flung network of waterways in the service of the Hudson Bay and Northwest Companies.

Although the Boundary Waters covers a huge area, the crowds seeking peace and solitude here are almost as large. The border lakes country is among our most popular, and thus overused, wildernesses. And as in many of our few remaining untamed landscapes, a simple tragedy of the commons is taking place here. Our rapidly increasing demand for wild land far exceeds the available supply. The unfortunate but unavoidable result is a compromised and degraded wilderness experience for everyone, and the situation will only get worse as more and more people try to squeeze into fewer and fewer acres, trying to find here what they can no longer find near their home.

When Mary and I applied for our camping permits in Grand Marais, the ranger issuing them warned us that most designated campsites would be filled by two in the afternoon at the latest and that we should plan on grabbing the first available site we saw, regardless of the time of day. His advice proved sound, and each day we found ourselves aced out of many campsites by groups staking claims shortly after noon.

The dying echo of metal on rock forces the issue. We're unwilling to engage in campsite competition, yet we're also frustrated by our inability to escape throngs of people just like ourselves—after all, we all came to the wilderness to get away from crowds. We look at each other and it's clear we're thinking the same thing. Without a word we get out the maps and examine our options.

At this small lake well off the main canoe routes we have found solitude and the companionship of wild creatures. But we know that the next lake, a large body of water speckled with numerous rock-rimmed islands, will probably be swarming with people. Unfolding the maps, we spread them out on our rocky summit and plot a new route, avoiding even marginally popular lakes. Rather than large swaths of blue, we look for the symbol indicating muskeg; rather than easy canoe routes, we look for portages. Satisfied with our plan, we pack up and go.

As the stiflingly hot and humid afternoon wears on, we find ourselves at the bottom of a muddy, lily pad–covered pond, looking for the outlet of a narrow stream. We find it hidden by tall grasses and reeds at the bottom of a shallow bay. Only six or eight feet wide and sometimes less, the little river uncoils like a snake as it slithers across a broad valley between parallel low rocky ridges.

The stream meanders through spruce bogs and beaver flows. Often the way is blocked by beaver dams. Sometimes there's a gap in the dam where the chuckling crystal water flows, and we guide the canoes up through these narrow slots. More often we must get out and drag the heavily laden boats across the tops of the dams. At frequent intervals side channels enter our stream and keep us guessing as to the correct route.

By mid-afternoon the heat is oppressive. Tall, pearly white thunderheads tower above us. Suddenly, a ferocious gust of wind blows our canoes sideways, and we fight to regain control of the boats as the blast hurls us across the water. Stroking with all our strength, we barely have time to secure the boats and get ourselves ashore before the storm smashes into us with a startling fury.

Behind camp, back in the woods, we locate a tall birch with a sturdy branch protruding about twenty feet off the ground—a perfect tree for hanging food out of the reach of the many black bears that haunt these woods and waters.

All around us lightning crackles, striking the nearby ridges. Thunder cracks and booms with the crashing sounds of battle. Torrents of rain slash down with such violence that we can barely see the tall white pines across the stream, bending to the breaking point before the gale. And then the wind increases. Great limbs crack like gunshots and fly to earth. The rain turns to hail, stoning us with stinging blows, churning the water into a swirling maelstrom, covering the ground with glistening white ice.

For an hour we huddle in our raingear as the storm rages. And then it's over; the clouds part and the sun comes out. The canoes are like bathtubs, filled with icy water. We empty the boats and get under way again, chastened by the power of the storm.

For mile after mile we ascend the twisting stream, our progress interrupted by more beaver dams and many portages around little rocky falls and rapids. The country is wild, the portages little-used, and we see no other people. On one carry trail we do see large, cylindrical animal droppings filled with pieces of hair and bone. Nearby the tracks of a large wolf are deeply imprinted on the muddy trail. At the take-out of another portage, we startle a large fisher eating crayfish on a boulder by the bank.

The next afternoon we emerge from the narrow confines of the stream and enter a blue lake sparkling in the August sunshine. There's a fresh breeze blowing from the north and not a cloud in the sky. The humidity is gone, the air is crisp, and with a brisk tailwind the canoes leap across the waves, trailing wakes and speeding toward the opposite shore where we've spied a perfect stopping place: a broad, rose-colored sandy beach backed up against a smooth, rocky shelf. After our two days of paddling muddy beaver flows and portaging rocky cliffs, the beach seems like a miraculous gift. Upon landing we jump in the water for a swim, wash off the mud from the last boggy portage, then lie down on the warm sand in the sunshine and enjoy a mid-afternoon nap. "There is no life so happy as a voyageur's life," I remind Mary before closing my eyes and drifting off.

An hour later we're on the water paddling to the next portage, at the end of which we find a little pond perhaps a hundred yards across, and then another portage, our fortieth in six days of travel. As the sun begins its long slow arc toward the western horizon, we place the canoes into yet another bay of yet another lake, then paddle into another expanding vista. Our map shows a campsite on a long, narrow peninsula sticking far out into the lake. If the map is correct, the camp will have sweeping views up and down the

waterway, with both morning and evening light. I point the canoe directly at the sun and, half blinded by the intense light, stroke toward the silhouetted tip of the point.

The camp is even better than the map suggests. It sits on a broad knoll screened from the water by conifers through which we have an excellent view over the water in every direction. The cool evening air soughs gently between the boughs and, best of all, there's a beach facing east for morning swims and another facing west for evening dips. Settling in, we hear something smashing through the woods across the water. We watch a bull moose appear at the edge of the forest, then wade into the water and swim across a broad arm of the lake.

Leaving the water, the moose crosses a timbered island, reenters on the other side, then swims the rest of the way to the far shore. The route is clearly a well-used game trail, for a little later a black bear makes the same trip in the opposite direction. Emerging from the water on the far side, the

The next afternoon we emerge from the narrow confines of the stream and enter a blue lake sparkling in the August sunshine.

*The stream
meanders through
spruce bogs and
beaver flows,
and the way
is frequently
blocked by
beaver dams.
Often, we must
get out and
drag the heavily
laden boats
across the tops
of the dams.*

bear shakes himself like a large furry dog, then slips silently into the conifers and disappears.

As night falls, with the food hanging safely in a tree, the canoes overturned and secured, the dinner pots washed and put away, we pull our camp chairs close by the fire. The sky glows orange, the water laps at the shore, and the fire snaps and dances. Far off across the water to the north we again hear the ghostly call of the loon—the wandering spirit of a dead warrior, according to the Cree. I listen until the echoes die, until the silence gathers around us, then open my well-worn copy of Sigurd Olson's classic tribute to the Boundary Waters, *The Singing Wilderness*, and read:

"There is magic in the feel of a paddle and the movement of a canoe, a magic compounded by distance, adventure, solitude, and peace. The way of a canoe is the way of the wilderness and of a freedom almost forgotten. It is an antidote to insecurity, the open door to waterways of ages past and a way of life with profound and abiding satisfactions. When a man is part of his canoe, he is part of all that canoes have ever known."

*The camp is even
better than the map
suggests. The cool
air soughs gently
between the boughs,
and we have an
excellent view over
the water in all
directions.*

RIVER

OF

GHOSTS

Upper Missouri National Wild and Scenic River, Montana

THE BOW OF MY SOLO CANOE slices the chocolate-brown water like a sharp knife, sending ripples purling gently to the shore. Kneeling in the center of the boat, I feel the Missouri River grab the hull and pull me swiftly toward a rough country of shattered cliffs and badlands. Deep, fractured coulees snake up into the high bluffs and jumbled hills beyond the river banks: the Missouri Breaks. The landscape is a maze of fissures—from the air it must look like the spiderweb cracks of a smashed windshield.

From Great Falls east toward the badlands of North Dakota, the Missouri cuts a deep, rugged gorge across the Montana high plains. Here, steep, eroded cliffs gouged by the river plummet a thousand feet from the canyon rim, revealing ten million years of geologic history. In places, epochs of wind and rain have washed away the sediments, exposing massive rock crags and dazzling white sandstone castles looming high above the river. The labyrinth of side canyons and coulees are rich in wildlife, including bighorn sheep and big-bodied mule deer bucks with broad sweeping racks. In the sky, bald and golden eagles ride the thermals while white pelicans skim the river surface in perfect flight formation.

We strike out on foot up the coulee to the bluffs above the river. Our route takes us past walls, columns, pillars, and weird weathered formations of pure white stone.

The Upper Missouri National Wild and Scenic River flows east for some 150 miles through some of the wildest, loneliest, and most historically significant stretches of open space in the lower forty-eight states. Dan and I begin our trip at the little outpost of Fort Benton, Montana, and plan to paddle downstream to the Charles M. Russell National Wildlife Refuge, where the swift, free-flowing river meets the impoundment of the giant Fort Peck Reservoir. For the next ten days or so, we'll literally go with the flow, riding the river through territory virtually unchanged for more than one hundred years. At the end of the twentieth century, this is still one of the greatest canoe trips in the world, a journey through time on the river of the Old West.

The Breaks and surrounding Plains were the home of buffalo-hunting Blackfeet, Assiniboin, and Crow Indians. Lewis and Clark traveled to the Pacific through the Breaks in the spring of 1805. Later, the Missouri was the water highway of the Mountain Men, the fur trappers who poled and paddled their pirogues upstream to reach the Rocky Mountain beaver country. Afterwards, rustlers, whiskey traders, and notorious outlaws including Butch Cassidy, the Sundance Kid, and Kid Curry found refuge in the inaccessible Breaks.

A lonesome weathered cabin sits in the middle of the empty windswept plain. Here, and at the many homesteads we'll pass in the days to come, the dream of Eden just didn't work out.

Late in the afternoon of our first day, we spot a perfect campsite at the head of an island in a big bend in the river. Soon we have a hot fire crackling and dinner pots simmering. Rich evening sunlight slides under dark ominous clouds, washing the cliffs in a lavish golden hue. I watch the yellow cottonwood flames for a while, then head for the tent. I take a last look at the sky and see a few stars twinkling through the ragged clouds racing high above, a promise of fair weather to come.

The next morning, we guide our canoes through a maze of islands and gravel bars. The Missouri is a wild river, undammed and unchanneled, and it meanders at will, creating new islands and bars that can confuse the pad-

dler. As we turn a corner, the wind is strong in our faces, and for the next several miles we fight our way downstream. The Missouri loops and bends like a snake, and we alternately go with the wind or struggle against it.

At noon we stop across the river from an expansive plain stretching north toward a set of jumbled hills. In 1832, the American Fur Company established a trading post here for the Blackfeet, Gros Ventre, and Kootenai. Named Fort McKenzie, it was the first successful trading venture to operate with the Blackfeet, a tribe extremely hostile to the Americans. Relations between the Americans and the Blackfeet were always tense, but in 1844 they erupted in great bloodshed. Ultimately, the Blackfeet burned the fort to the ground, driving the Americans out of the region and forcing them to

It's impossible to enter these abandoned homesteads and not feel the presence of the former owners. But there's no one here now, no one but the ghosts.

relocate many miles downstream at the mouth of the Judith River. Today, the site of Fort McKenzie is still called Brule (burned) Bottom.

We get back in the canoes and thread our way through a maze of islands. As we pass, the sky fills with angry, scolding flocks of geese and ducks. Though the surrounding breaks are dry and covered with sagebrush, the river corridor is teeming with life. The rings of rising fish dapple the water before our canoes, and often when we look up to the cliffs and hills, we see bands of mule deer climbing in single file across the steep slopes.

Late in the afternoon of our second day on the river, as Dan and I approach the mouth of a tributary flowing in from the north, we recall that the fate of the Corps of Discovery depended upon Lewis and Clark making the right choice at this critical juncture. The men of the expedition were convinced that the north fork was the Missouri, while the captains felt that the south fork was the route to the Pacific. The expedition camped here from June 2 through June 11 while they determined which fork to take.

Lewis took a small group of men to ascend the north fork for several days and determined that it could not possibly be the Missouri. Returning to camp at the forks, he named the tributary Maria's River in honor of his cousin Miss Maria Wood.

The Missouri turns to the east, and with a mostly fair wind and clear skies, we are reluctant to stop paddling. We cover some twenty-two river miles before pulling over to an island where we make camp at sunset. Throughout the night I hear the cries of agitated geese and once, off in the distance, the high-pitched wail of a coyote.

The next afternoon, we paddle up a creek flowing in from the north. A gentle ridge leads to the skyline, and with a couple of hours of sunlight remaining, we take a break from canoeing and hike up to the canyon rim. Picking our way through prickly pear cactus and sagebrush, we climb a couple of hundred feet up on the cliffs. From up here the Missouri looks like a giant snake, slithering across sere badlands toward the horizon. Off in the distance, a mountain range—the Bears Paw—rises above a vast stretch of dry, empty plains.

As we hike along the rim, we learn we aren't the first to visit this barren ridge. At first we see only vast distance and bleak emptiness, but when we look closer, dozens of stone rings appear lying undisturbed, scattered in the grass across the bluff. In the center of some there is a depression scooped out of the dry soil. These stones were used to hold down the buffalo robes that covered tepees; the depressions are fire pits in the center of the lodges. We're walking through an Indian encampment that has rested here undisturbed for over a century.

Descending to the river and camp, I linger in a stone circle sitting off by itself at the tip of a long, narrow ridge. This ring is a hundred feet below the others, out of sight of the main Indian camp, but with a good overview of the creek and river valleys below. I imagine a sentry keeping watch on the creek and the river from here. Or perhaps this was a special ceremonial site. In any event, it's a peaceful spot with a tremendous view, and just as I'm about to get up and wander back down to the cottonwood trees lining the river, six deer emerge from a narrow gulch directly below. They walk through the sage to the trees in single file and disappear.

At dawn two days later, we kindle a fire of dry beaver-gnawed sticks, cook breakfast, and watch the sun poke over the bone-white sandstone cliffs to the east. It's a chilly morning and I'm wearing a ski hat, gloves, and lots of warm clothes as I huddle near the flames. Dan is flipping through a copy of the *Journals of Lewis & Clark*.

"Hey," he says, "listen to what Lewis wrote when they were camped in this exact spot."

"As we passed on," Dan reads, "it seemed as if those scenes of visionary enchantment would never have an end; for here it is too that nature presents to the view of the traveler vast ranges of walls of tolerable workmanship, so perfect indeed are those walls that I should have thought that nature had attempted here to rival the human art of masonry. . . ."

As the sun warms the land, we leave the canoes and strike out on foot up the broad valley of Eagle Creek. The route takes us past columns, pillars, and weird weathered formations of pure white stone. Some of the stones scattered across the outwash plain have been worn over time to perfect spheres the size and shape of cannonballs. Above and all around us, cliffs of white sandstone have eroded through the eons and now resemble buildings, amphitheaters, and castle battlements. We share the captains' amazement at the handiwork of nature.

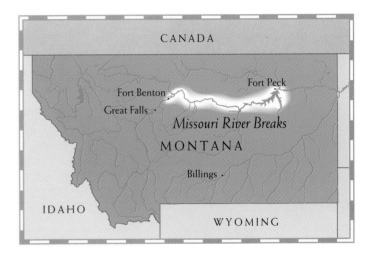

Back at the river, we get under way, battling a fierce headwind through the White Cliffs. The miles slip under our hulls until, late that afternoon, we reach a broad bend with a sagebrush bench sweeping back up into the treeless Breaks. A lonesome weathered cabin sits in the middle of the empty windswept plain. There was once a homestead here at this desolate spot, in the middle of the Great American Desert. Who lived here, we wonder, and what brought them to this particular place?

In 1909, the Homestead Act was enlarged, allowing people to file on 320 acres, double the original allotment. The expanded act touched off Montana's homestead boom, and in the years just prior to World War I and continuing through the 1920s, thousands who had never handled a plow or seen the hind quarters of a horse flocked to Montana in search of their agrarian dreams. They envisioned Montana's high plains as a Garden of Eden, a breadbasket waiting for the plow to unleash its riches. Today all that remains are the weathered and worn cabins. Poor soils, brutal cold, extreme heat, hail, hoppers, and drought sent the homesteaders reeling in defeat. At the end of the twentieth century, the river is lonelier than it has been since Lewis and Clark passed through.

The next day we spot a ranch house on the right bank, the first occupied dwelling we've seen in days. We pull over, then stop to look around. Vintage cars share a pasture with tractors, combines, and harvesting machines dating from the turn of the century to modern times. The massive rolling irrigation system is disconnected. Strangely, the fences are down and the gates are open. It's spring planting season but there are no green shoots rising from the fields. The windows in the house are intact, but the shades are drawn.

Dan knocks on the door. Silence. We look at each other. Okay, now what? I turn the handle and the door opens. "Hello!" I shout. But there's nobody home, and whoever lived here packed up and left in a hurry. There are still clothes in the closets, cans and boxes of food in the cabinets, empty bottles on the tables, old stubbed out cigarettes in the ashtrays.

I examine a pile of magazines in the living room and some scattered letters in the bedroom. The most recent are dated 1983. That's when whoever lived here finally went bust. We leave everything as we found it, shut the door, and head back to the canoes. At another abandoned ranch downstream, the scene is repeated, except this time the newspapers and magazines date from 1949. A rusting Chevy waits patiently out front, a tractor sits under the sun where it was left on that last sad day. But there's no one here to turn the key—no one but the ghosts watching us from the upstairs window. Here, the dream of Eden just didn't work out.

Late in the afternoon of day six, near the mouth of the Judith River, we spot a lone ranch set back a half mile from the river. Green, irrigated hayfields suggest this ranch has not been abandoned to the ghosts. While I set up camp, Dan hikes off to see if anyone's home. Sometime later I hear the growl of a pickup truck in low gear, and soon I'm shaking the enormous gnarled hand of Jerry Halter, the son of a homesteader and a man who has worked his own place here in the Judith country for over fifty years.

On the far side of seventy, a World War II veteran who fought in the Pacific, Jerry looks like the Marlboro Man in his later years. With sun-creased brow, flowing white mustache, and bowlegged walk, he personifies this rugged landscape. There's a rifle on the dashboard of the truck and a whiskey bottle under the seat. He ushers us into the beat-up GMC and bounces us over the sagebrush plain to the ranch, where he tells us to make ourselves at home.

As we hike along the rim, we learn we aren't the first to visit this barren ridge. Dozens of stone tepee rings lie undisturbed in the grass.

From here Lewis caught his first glimpse of what he thought were the Rockies. "While I viewed these mountains," he wrote, "I felt a secret pleasure in finding myself so near the head of the heretofore conceived boundless Missouri."

Sitting under the watchful gaze of a dozen deer and elk heads, we talk through the night. Jerry spins stories of the early days at Judith Landing, of outlaws and Indians, Lewis and Clark, steamboats and ranches. He holds us spellbound.

Of all the crossroads on the northern Plains, the mouth of the Judith was probably the most significant. Judith Landing was the site of important peace conferences between the Plains Indians and American envoys in 1846 and again in 1855. The army maintained a post here, and a battle was fought with the Sioux in 1868. A major Blackfeet war trail led through here south to Crow country.

As we sip another cup of strong coffee, Jerry shows us a collection of artifacts he's found around the ranch—gun barrels, horseshoes, and a "running iron" used by rustlers to change cattle and horse brands. "If you were found carrying one of these," says Jerry, passing the iron ring to me, "you were hanged on the spot."

The next morning I help Jerry load some cattle into a trailer, then we head our separate ways—Jerry to auction in Great Falls, Dan and I downstream through the most rugged section of the journey, the region the early French trappers called *Les Mauvaises Terres*—the Bad Lands.

"The Missouri was a devil of a river," wrote A. B. Guthrie in *The Big Sky*. "It was a rolling wall . . . it was no river at all but a great loose water that leaped from the mountains and tore through the plains, wild to get to the sea."

And it still is. Two days later, as we paddle through the Bad Lands, the river pushes with an intensity we haven't felt before, and a strong upstream wind blows fiercely, creating big choppy waves that threaten to spill over our sides and swamp the boats.

We enjoy every minute. The bright sunshine flashes on the water as the canoes ride the waves of Lone Pine, Castle Bluff, and Magpie Rapids. By noon we're at the lip of Bird Rapids, where the Missouri picks up speed sweeping around a big bend beneath a towering rock reef. Pulling over to the north shore for a lunch break, we tie the canoes and hike up to a warm sandy ledge.

Directly across the river from us is a broad sagebrush bench at the base of a timbered ridge. Lewis and Clark camped there on May 26, 1805. For all appearances, they might have camped there last night—the site looks as it must have on that very significant day.

Earlier on the 26th, Lewis hiked up into the breaks above Bullwhacker Creek. "On arriving to the summit [of] one of the highest points in the

From the Great Falls of Montana east toward the Dakota Badlands, the Missouri River cuts a deep, rugged gorge across the high plains.

neighborhood I thought myself well repaid for my labour; as from this point I beheld the Rocky Mountains for the first time," he wrote.

In the afternoon of our ninth day, Dan and I make camp in an airy grove of cottonwoods at the mouth of Bullwhacker Creek, then set out on foot along a game trail, perhaps the very one Lewis took into the high country. After some hard hiking we ascend the highest point, likely the pinnacle Lewis stood upon, and are rewarded with an expansive view of the Judith and Bears Paw Mountains—outlying ranges of the Rockies. "While I viewed these mountains," Lewis wrote, "I felt a secret pleasure in finding myself so near the head of the heretofore conceived boundless Missouri."

Traveling in the opposite direction, 200 years later, we too are nearing the end of our journey. And yet time seems to matter little here in the Breaks. In the morning, when we pass two large bands of bighorn sheep clinging to the sheer shale walls, we are again reminded how much we share with the captains.

*Dan Berns paddles
through the White
Cliffs. "As we
passed on," Lewis
wrote, "it seemed
as if those seens
[sic] of visionary
inchantment [sic]
would never have
and [sic] end."*

"As we ascended the river today," Lewis wrote on May 25, "I saw several gangs of the bighorned animals on the face of the steep bluffs and cliffs . . . sent Drewyer to kill one which he accomplished . . . the head and horns of the male which Drewyer killed weighed 27 Lbs." Eerily, the next time Dan and I pull over to shore, we nearly trip upon the skeleton and massive horns of a mature bighorn ram.

Two days later, we spot a major stream flowing in from the north. Securing the canoes, we hike across a cactus-studded plain to the hidden entrance of a steep-sided canyon. There's an old but well-defined path here, as if generations of buffalo, horse, and cattle had passed this way. Taking a long pull on our water bottles, we start up Hideaway Coulee under a blazing sun.

Hideaway Coulee is where the outlaw Kid Curry sought refuge from the law. Butch Cassidy, the Sundance Kid, and the Hole-in-the-Wall Gang came up from Wyoming in 1901, joining Curry here for one of the last train

OVERLEAF:
*The landscape is a
rough country of
rugged cliffs and
badlands. Deep frac-
tured coulees snake
up into the high
bluffs and shattered
hills beyond the
riverbanks.*

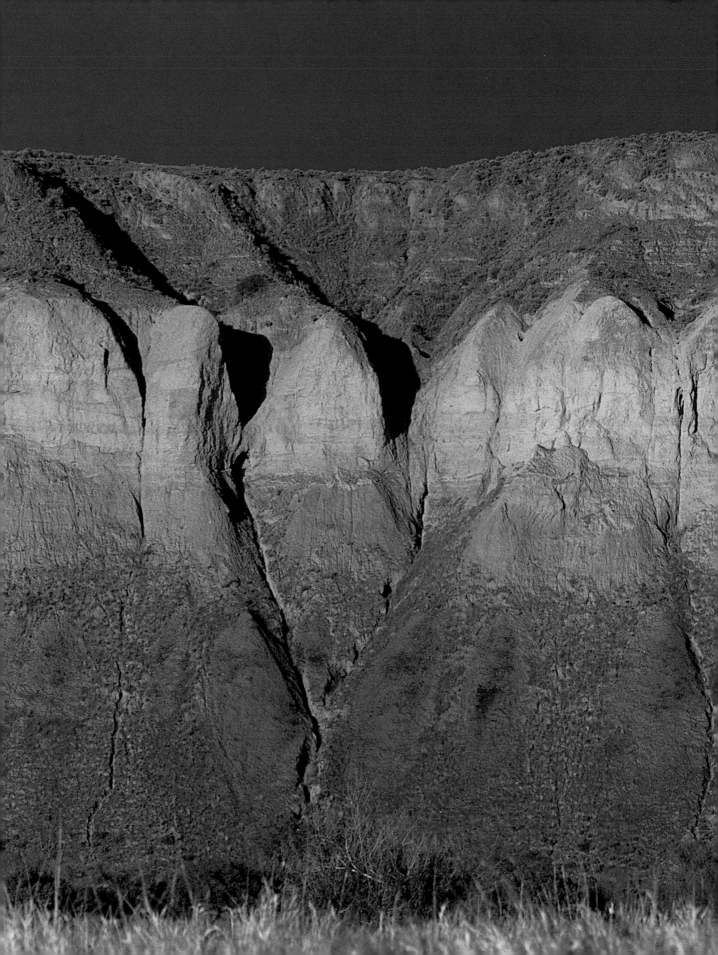

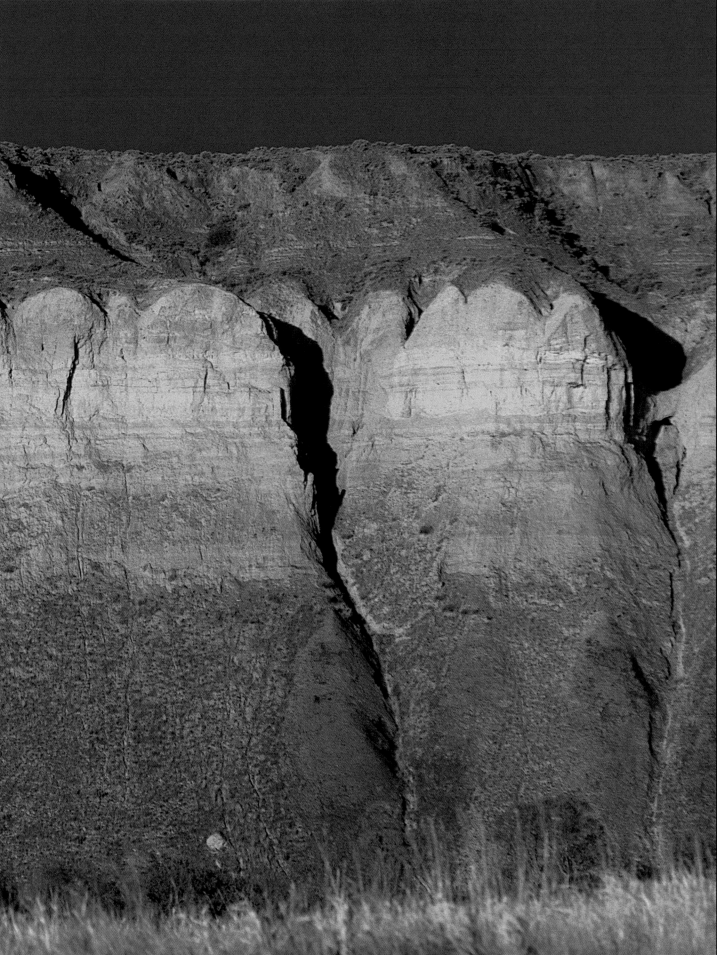

holdups in the United States, when the outlaws robbed the Great Northern near the railroad siding of Wagner.

Jerry Halter, whose father knew the engineer on that train, told us, "When the sun is at the right angle, you can still see glass shimmering in the sagebrush where Butch and those boys blew the safe." The gang fled here, to Hideaway Coulee before escaping to Bolivia, where supposedly they were shot and killed in 1911.

"Those boys weren't killed in South America," Jerry insisted. "Butch changed his name and moved to Spokane, Washington. People around here still remember him driving up in that big fancy Cadillac, visiting his old stomping grounds back in the 1930s." The countryside around Hideaway Coulee is so rugged that for all we know old Butch is up here still.

A vintage automobile waits patiently under the Montana sun in the Missouri Breaks for its owner to return and drive away, a silent testimony to homesteaders' dreams that were not to be.

Of all the sights we've seen on the river, of all the places where people's dreams unfolded or were crushed by forces beyond their control, the most poignant is the battlefield at Cow Island Landing where Chief Joseph and the Nez Perce crossed the river on their tragic 1,200-mile flight from Oregon to Canada in 1877.

After more than four months of fighting a defensive campaign, the fugitive Nez Perce reached Cow Island on September 23, 1877. Here, the beleaguered Indians found 50 tons of freight and supplies at the steamboat landing, guarded by a detachment of United States soldiers. After offering to purchase supplies and being refused, the Nez Perce attacked. There was fierce fighting in the rocks and bluffs as the soldiers dug in and the Indians charged. While the soldiers were pinned down in their rifle pits, the Nez Perce took what they could carry and burned the rest.

Just two weeks later, Chief Joseph and most of the Nez Perce (a handful snuck across the border to join Sitting Bull's Sioux in exile) were captured by General Nelson Miles just north of the Bears Paw Mountains, a mere 45 miles from the Canadian border and freedom. On October 5, 1877, Joseph handed his rifle to Miles and said, "Hear me my chiefs. I am

tired; my heart is sick and sad. From where the sun now stands, I will fight no more forever."

Dan and I walk the battlefield at Cow Island and imagine the Nez Perce coming over the ridge, riding down the coulee and into the river canyon. Across the years we can sense their desperation and the fear of the blue-clad soldiers as the shots rained down from the rocks above. As we walk along, we find deep, symmetrical depressions in the earth. Grown in now but unmistakable, these are the rifle pits where the soldiers survived at least three charges during the night before reinforcements arrived from Fort Benton.

I lie down and take a prone firing position in a rifle pit where a soldier surely positioned himself on that day in 1877. The view over the rim is essentially unchanged, and as I have so many other times on this long and eventful journey, I feel as though I'm in the company of ghosts.

Dan Berns hurries to secure his canoe as a violent thunderstorm approaches.

HIGH
C O U N T R Y
S N O W S

Grand Teton National Park, Wyoming

'M AWAKE BEFORE DAWN'S PALE LIGHT glows in the east.
The sky is thick and fuzzy, the color and texture of my old wool socks, and
a fresh skein of dry powder snow covers everything. Snug in my sleeping
bag at the bottom of a narrow snow trench, "Steve's snow coffin," as Mary
calls my preferred lightweight disposable shelter, I feel a cool wind flowing
down from the flanks of Housetop Mountain, the serrated peak looming
like a frosted wedding cake above our camp at Marion Lake, high on the
Teton Crest in Wyoming.

Spruce boughs rustle above me, then a sharp gust flings a stinging blast
of icy spindrift in my face. Any thoughts of idly lying around, waiting for
someone to bring me my morning coffee, quickly scatter with the breeze.

We break camp at sunrise, or what would be sunrise if we could see
the sun, and begin the climb out of the North Fork of Granite Canyon.
Carrying fifty-pound packs and sliding on telemark skis fitted with climbing skins, we follow the tracks that Jay Pistono, friend, professional ski
mountaineer, and the third member of our party had cut across the featureless snow plain the previous evening, anticipating just such near-whiteout
conditions.

"Gives you vertigo," says Jay with a grin as we kick and glide. "Like
skiing inside a milk bottle."

The clouds vanish as the route climbs toward a divide. Soon only tat-
tered shreds of vapor are snagged on the sharpest peaks, and bright
sunshine strikes out of the clean blue sky. Intense white light bounces off
the snow, and I reposition my glacier glasses to block the blinding rays. The
temperature, which had been in the high twenties, soars through the fifties,
but it feels much hotter. Stripping off shell gear, we peel down to a single
layer of clothing and sunscreen. All around us sharp sedimentary crags with
names like Spearhead Peak stab the sky.

*Atop Hurricane
Pass, Jay Pistono
stands beneath the
chiseled pinnacle of
the Grand Teton. The
towering gray spire is
virtually in our laps.
If someone were
climbing that granite
blade, I'm sure we
could carry on a
conversation, maybe
even shake hands.*

69

A short climb brings us to the crest of Fox Creek Pass. There, towering above us to the left, vertical cliffs rise up and out of sight. To the right, sheer walls plunge down into the gaping chasm of Death Canyon, named for a surveyor who disappeared there in 1903. But stretching straight ahead of us in the direction we want to go is one of the miracles of Teton ski mountaineering: Death Canyon Shelf—a wide, nearly level ledge cutting a perfect skier's highway straight across the precipitous cliffs—stretches all the way to Mount Meek Pass three miles to the north.

"How's that for a pretty sight?" says Jay. "The route just keeps rolling along."

Seen from Jackson Hole, Wyoming, the Tetons are an imposing range, a striking wall of mountains with almost mythic qualities. Their classic profile is among the most stunning sights in the world. Scorning foothills, the Tetons erupt 7,000 feet straight up from the Snake River plain to scratch the firmament with sharp, triangular snowcapped spires, six of which top out above 12,000 feet. Not surprisingly, the Tetons have lured the world's best mountaineers. Nathaniel P. Langford, later Yellowstone National Park's first superintendent, claimed the summit of the Grand Teton in 1872.

Spectacular as they are, at first glance the Tetons don't conjure visions of long backcountry ski treks. Rather the opposite, in fact. The Tetons are home to the Jackson Hole ski resort, which rightly boasts more heart-pounding double-black-diamond runs per acre than anywhere else on earth. Short of a series of death-defying ups and downs, there doesn't appear to be any way to traverse the range.

But there is, and it's one of ski mountaineering's greatest trips.

Here's the secret: the Tetons are a false-front range, roughly twenty miles wide by fifty miles long, gouged with deep canyons separating the peaks. These canyons—Granite, Death, Cascade—reach far back behind the highest peaks. Thus the actual crest of the range and the ski route along it, is behind the mountain front, atop the divide separating Grand Teton National Park and the Jedediah Smith Wilderness in Targhee National Forest.

The Tetons are the newest mountains in the Rockies. Fifty million years younger than the nearby Wind River Range, the Tetons were formed about ten million years ago, when the earth's crust cracked along a sharply angled fault. That fault still lies along the base of the mountains in Jackson Hole, which is dropping like a trapdoor (in geologic time, at least, though scientists say slips of up to ten feet are possible anytime). As the valley falls, the precipitous mountain front continues to rise.

The result of all this lifting and sinking is a classic fault-block range, precisely the kind of mountain architecture ideal for long-distance ski

That night we camped in the trees, looking up Cascade Canyon at the snowy summits gleaming in the last light of day.

tours. Ski mountaineers of all levels can stay high among the peaks while threading a route through them, using a meandering network of connecting high plateaus, glaciated bowls, and providentially placed passages such as Death Canyon Shelf.

Because of these concealed bowls and shelves, the skiing is more moderate and more continuous than might be expected in such a rugged, high-altitude setting. Add to this sweet mixture long periods of warm, dry air between the monstrous snowstorms that build up a 500-inch base by springtime, and the result is a multi-day ski mountaineering tour through some of the world's finest high alpine scenery.

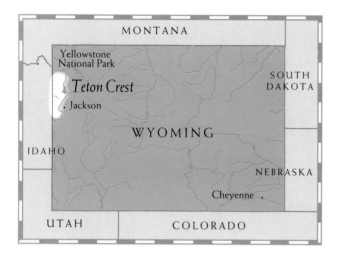

For advanced experts and adrenaline junkies, the Teton Crest Traverse also stashes a trove of moderate to extreme steeps. And because it's such an intricate range, the options for side trips and route variations are virtually limitless. This is a place that begs to be skied, and though mountaineers have been pioneering ski routes in the Tetons since the 1930s, every tour here feels like a journey into the unknown.

The Teton Crest Traverse began for us in Jackson, Wyoming, the quirky little cow-cum-tourist town at the southern end of the Tetons. The first homesteaders and ranchers arrived here in the mid-1880s to graze cattle and raise hay. But it didn't take too many Wyoming winters before the locals realized there was more money to be made wrangling dudes and catering to wealthy sportsmen than in grazing cattle at 6,200 feet. Now home to movie stars, celebrities, and trust-fund kids, Jackson is viewed with a mixture of disgust and envy by the rest of Wyoming—sometimes you get the feeling that other parts of the self-styled Cowboy State would rather deny that Jackson even exists.

We'd planned a five-day tour along the crest, covering about fifty miles. Before we started, Mary and I spent a day getting acclimated by exploring the expansive snow bowls easily accessed by driving a few short miles up Teton Pass. There we rallied with Polly and Sandy Wakeman, Mainers spending the winter sniffing out powder shots throughout the

Tetons. A former member of the U.S. telemark racing team, Polly showed off her nimble touch by linking perfect garlands straight down the fresh face of Edelweiss Bowl. Sandy, with a more muscular style, roared down the slope, stopping only when his stamina gave out and he augured into the bottomless white. We ended the day by telemarking down Chivers Ridge to the abandoned Old Pass Road, first skied by turn-of-the-century couriers carrying the mail over the mountains between Wyoming and Idaho. The unplowed road plunged down the mountain for about five miles before dropping us in the little village of Wilson at the Stagecoach Bar, where we toasted our efforts with a few rounds of Snake River Ale.

The next morning we met Jay on Teton Pass and began our tour in earnest. We shouldered our packs under perfect skies and began skinning up the long, gradual approach to our first hurdle, Phillips Pass.

Jay was out front setting the pace, breaking trail in the soft spring snow and picking a route through the trailless forest. This is not as easy as it

At tree line we found a protected spot with a wide-open view over Moose Creek and a string of unnamed 10,000-foot peaks to the west. Already the sky was flaming orange.

sounds, for any summer trail markings along the crest are buried under dozens of feet of snow in winter. Skiers attempting the traverse should be proficient at map and compass work or should enlist the aid of a knowledgeable guide like Jay. Not only did Jay pick the safest course time after time, he also saved us hours of unnecessary climbing by always choosing the highest route possible. He called this "wrapping a traverse" or "flowing a passage," and the lines he chose were truly artistic.

We climbed gradually, every now and then emerging from the trees into blinding white light. The day was approaching hot, and within a few hours we were beyond parched. We stopped often to drink, each time refilling our water bottles with wet snow. Once, while traversing above a snowy meadow, we looked down upon a set of bear tracks the size of dinner plates. The grizzlies were already emerging from their winter dens, and we speculated about meeting a bear on our tour.

Late that afternoon we crested Phillips Pass and stayed high, wrapping around the west side of Rendezvous Peak. Right at tree line we found a protected spot with a wide-open view over Moose Creek and a string of unnamed 10,000-foot peaks to the west. Already the sky was flaming orange. Quitting time. We dropped packs and made a high camp under the stars.

The next morning we packed up and started out under sapphire skies once again. A short traverse led to an immaculate 500-foot drop of perfect powder cantilevered at about a forty-degree pitch. We checked our avalanche beacons, secured pack straps and jacket cuffs, then plunged in one at a time, cautiously but eagerly ripping three squiggly lines in the fresh powder. We dumped our packs at the bottom, then skinned back up and figure-eighted our own tracks.

If you've never done it, skiing wild snow with your house on your back is very different from schussing on-piste at the resorts. When you sink into your turn, the tendency is to keep sinking, and when you rise up out of your perfectly carved arc, you might as well have an anvil on your back. Certain adjustments are in order: minimize the up-down, and pay attention to fore-aft and lateral stability. When a fifty-to-sixty pound backpack gets going, it wants to keep on going and take you with it.

But this hauling of all life's necessities with you, this enforced self-sufficiency, is another thing that makes the Teton Crest so challenging. Unlike on Europe's Haute Route or Colorado's Tenth Mountain Trail, routes where you can travel in relative luxury from hut-to-hut with a day pack, on the

Jay was out front setting the pace, breaking trail in the soft spring snow. We climbed gradually, every now and then emerging from the trees into the blinding white light.

ski the crest between December and March, months when heavy snowfall is an almost daily occurrence and the avalanche danger is high. Now, in mid-March, we are a little ahead of the prime season, and looking up, I am slightly apprehensive.

Jay instructs us to keep about a hundred yards apart and "go like hell." Fortunately the shelf is slightly downhill, and by skating and tucking we cover a couple of miles in a matter of minutes. Near the middle of the shelf there is an enormous boulder the size of a large house, and we stop to rest and drink some water before scampering safely to Meek Pass at the end of the shelf.

Meek Pass is named for mountain man Joe Meek, who was already a grizzled veteran of the fur trade at the tender age of twenty-two when the annual Rendezvous, or trapper's fair, was held in Idaho's Teton Valley in 1832. The highlight of the Rendezvous that year was a pitched battle between the mountain men and the local Gros Ventre Indians, who shared this country with the Snake Indians. The river at the base of the Tetons is named for these Native Americans, not for the reptile.

You can't travel far in the Tetons without crossing the tracks of the mountain men, those peripatetic loners who knew every pass and every stream from the Gila to the Judith. The first non-Indian to venture into the Tetons was John Colter, who crossed the range twice during the winter of 1807–8. The greatest mountain man of them all, Jim Bridger, was thoroughly familiar with the Teton country, and he named Jackson Hole in honor of his friend and partner, Davey Jackson, who loved this high mountain valley. The Tetons themselves were named by a group of French Canadian trappers sometime in the early 1800s. It's not hard to imagine them staring up at those suggestive peaks and murmuring, *"Ah, les trois tétons!"* (Ah, the three tits!)

As we crest Meek Pass they come fully into view—South, Middle, and Grand Teton, the Cathedral Group—soaring in the clear dry air, so close we can see every crack and fissure of their tapering, ice-crusted spires. It is an awesome sight, and for the next few minutes we stare, transfixed, trying to grasp the scene before us before dropping off the pass and wrapping a high traverse into Alaska Basin, a huge glacier-cut bowl.

We celebrate our solitude by making a quick camp, then skiing some wide-open, low-angle slopes that turn a deep orange as the sun drops below the rim of Battleship Mountain.

According to *The Hiker's Guide to Wyoming,* trips into Alaska Basin are not encouraged due to the heavy use the area incurs. That may be so in summer, but we haven't seen any sign of humanity on the crest, nor will we for the duration of the trek, and as we descend into the basin there isn't another soul in sight, not even an old track. Our only witnesses are the silent snow-cloaked mountains and passes of the interior Teton Range. We celebrate our solitude by making a quick camp, then skiing some wide-open, low-angle slopes, which turn a deep orange hue as the sun drops below the rim of Battleship Mountain. That night the white contrail of the Hale-Bopp Comet races across the indigo sky, high above the shining mountains.

On another perfect morning we lounge in camp under a blue vault of sky, soaking up the warm sunshine. The climb out of Alaska Basin to the summit of Hurricane Pass is the steepest of the tour, and we justify our slow start by convincing each other that our sleeping bags need airing out. But soon we are skinning up the side of the bowl, sweating like racehorses. The snow-plastered basin gathers the sunlight and bounces it back at us like a gigantic solar oven. The terrain steepens near the top and we take off our skis, kicking steps up to the lip. At the summit I'm sucking wind and my eyes are stinging with sweat. But that's okay because directly across from us in the clean, calm air are the chiseled pinnacles of the Tetons, the towering gray spires virtually in our laps. If someone were climbing those granite blades I'm sure we could carry on a conversation, maybe even shake hands. Spellbound, barely able to avert our gazes, we loaf in the sunshine atop the misnamed pass, the scenic high point of the traverse.

Ski mountaineering is tough. The price of all this beauty is sweat and aching muscles. The trick is to let the rhythm of motion and the bewitching scenery work their magic.

Skiers who have never shouldered a pack on a high country tour may well question the sanity of those who set out on fifty-mile forced marches through the wilderness. To be sure, the Teton Crest *is* hard: hazards abound, and every one of those miles is paid for with a certain amount of pain and suffering. But the intoxicating beauty of the world at 10,000 feet more than makes up for any discomfort, and from Hurricane Pass to the northern end of the route at Jenny Lake, the skiing is all downhill.

We spill over a sixty-degree headwall and slash down to Schoolroom Glacier at the head of the South Fork of Cascade Canyon. With the Tetons

directly above us we speed down the twisting white tongue of snow on the canyon floor. Fully exposed to catastrophic slide paths, we race past the danger zone, keeping an eye on the loaded snow walls above while maintaining terminal velocity. We yield to gravity's pull for three or four miles until we hit the main drainage of Cascade Canyon, where we regroup in a speed- and danger-induced euphoria. That night we camp in the trees once more, looking up the gunsight notch of Valhalla Canyon toward the ice-spackled summits of the Grand Teton and Mount Owen.

Our final morning, we rocket down the canyon as it pitches and rolls like a luge run, careening around turns and dodging through trees. Too soon the canyon spills out of the mountains and drops us on the frozen shores of Jenny Lake.

In a couple of hours the trip will be over. But not yet. The Tetons still tower above us, and I can scarcely take my eyes from them as we skate down the gentle grade alongside Cottonwood Creek to the trailhead.

Mary Gorman and Jay Pistono are dwarfed by the massive shoulders of Housetop Mountain as they ascend above the North Fork of Granite Canyon.

PACKROD
PARADISE

Greater Yellowstone Region High Country, Wyoming and Montana

THE LATE AFTERNOON SUN turned the rocky ridge across the lake incandescent as I retrieved a little green, gold-beaded nymph with short, sharp strips. I had picked up the fly down in Cooke City, at the insistence of the guide manning the shop. He assured me the cutthroats up on the Beartooth Plateau would find it irresistible, so I stuck a few in my fly wallet and headed up into the hills.

The surface of the little lake, snowbound at its far end even in summer, was dimpled with the expanding ripples of feeding trout. In fact, if a flawless deep blue dome hadn't been stretched tight overhead, I'd have sworn it was raining. But while Dan Berns had already landed a neat succession of fifteen-inch cutts, my creel was empty. I tied on the secret weapon, took a low, crouching position behind a boulder, and made a pretty fair presentation ahead of the swirl not too far from the shoreline.

We entered a zone of alpine vegetation where the grass was bright green and the wildflowers abounded. The scene was a riot of color.

I felt a quick, electric pulse as the line came alive, and I tightened up. But as I did, the trout lunged and spit the hook. The line went dead, the connection broken. I spent the rest of the evening hours, as I so often do, watching Dan coax fish out of the water with an artist's master touch. Make no mistake. With his bushy beard and "new" fly outfit he picked up at a pawnshop in Bozeman years ago, he's no dilettante. No $400 Gore-Tex waders for him when a $5 pair of army surplus khakis will do. He calls what he does "callin' in the hogs." Personally, I think he's watched too many Saturday morning fishing shows.

The hogs were coming in, though. We'd have trout for supper again that night. I forgot about my empty creel and busied myself putting up the tent and getting a hot fire crackling down to a bed of glowing coals. As the sun set, a cool breeze flowed off the permanent snowfields high above and a blizzard of stars appeared out of the blackness. In a timeless ritual, we were

soon gnawing on fresh trout like corncobs, our greasy fingers and dripping chins glistening in the firelight.

That's the kind of primitive effect the Beartooth Mountains, themselves barely emerged from the Ice Age, can have on you. This is one of the West's highest, wildest regions, a phantasmagoric Pleistocene landscape where it's easy to believe giant cave bears still roam.

There may be taller mountain ranges in the West, and it's possible there's better fishing somewhere out here, but nowhere else is there a range with the combination of appeals that makes the Beartooths so unique. The open, parklike terrain, speckled with a multitude of trout-filled lakes and surrounded by chiseled mountains, makes this a packrod paradise. With a protected wilderness core of a million acres, there's simply no finer wandering in the West, and to hike along here, fly rod in hand, is a rare and wonderful privilege.

Rising beyond the northeast boundary of Yellowstone National Park, the Beartooth Mountains straddle the border between Wyoming and Montana for some 65 miles. Alternately covered by lava flows from Yellowstone's many eruptions and by thick glaciers, the Beartooths were formed by fire and ice. Characterized by steep mountains and rugged alpine cirques, this is the largest contiguous land mass above 10,000 feet in the United States. The mountain names—Froze-to-Death, Tempest, Spirit, Thunder, Bears Tooth—are testimony to the harsh splendor of the landscape.

What is most striking about this austere alpine expanse is the incredible amount of water it contains. Because of the plateau's east-west orientation, the Beartooths receive considerably less direct sun than other ranges. The winter snows melt later in the year, the runoff takes longer, and the range remains wetter throughout the short summer.

Up here there are snowfields and glaciers, perennial streams, wetlands and meadows, and more than a thousand clear, cool alpine lakes. Half of the lakes contain fish—cutthroat, golden, rainbow, and brook trout as well as grayling. As you hike, it's not uncommon to have seven or eight lakes in sight at one time.

The Beartooth sojourn began for Dan, Mary, my dog Tasha, and me in Cooke City. Cradled between the Beartooth and Absaroka Mountains, Cooke City is home to about a hundred year-round residents, most of whom make their living in various outdoors-related occupations. During the fleeting summer, roughly late July to early September, Cooke City serves as the northeastern gateway to Yellowstone, and the main street sees a steady stream of recreational vehicles and wide-eyed tourists. But during the long winter, the town virtually shuts down. Its only tenuous connection to the outside world is the road to Mammoth Hot Springs, clear across the northern range of the park.

Because of its end-of-the-road status, Cooke has everything an adventurous traveler could need or want, from the little gold-beaded nymph to a cold pint of Scapegoat Ale to slake your thirsty pipes. There's one other important advantage to embarking on your Beartooth journey from Cooke City—if you follow the Beartooth Highway out of town for about an hour or so, you can begin your hike at 9,500 feet, up at tree line, eliminating a couple of days of serious uphill slogging from other trailheads down in the valleys below.

We left the truck at Island Lake, an achingly beautiful body of blue water surrounded by a fantastic tableau of ice, looming rocky ridges, and cobalt sky. The trail followed the shoreline, then skirted a belt of sub-alpine fir where we watched a moose cow and calf wade across a boggy meadow. Leaving the spindly picket line of trees behind, we entered a zone of alpine vegetation that swept up the steep sides of the peaks until it gave way to crumbly rock and scree slopes high above. Here the grass was as smooth and green as a golf course. Wildflowers abounded. The Beartooths are home to

OVERLEAF:
Distant glaciers and snowfields seemed just beyond reach. Unable to still his twitching casting hand, Dan fell several lakes behind. We could see him tossing graceful arcs of line out across the water toward the concentric swirls of hungry fish.

some 386 plant species—the richest flora of any mountain range in the country—and the scene was a riot of color.

The air was so transparent we could see fracture lines on mountains fifty miles away. Distant glaciers and snowfields seemed just beyond reach. Cool currents of mountain air washed down from the heights, riffling the surfaces of the lakes. Following the thin trail across the open country, we made good time. We passed Night Lake, Flake Lake, Jeff Lake, and a handful of others without names. Unable to still his twitching casting hand, Dan fell several lakes behind. We could sometimes see him back in the distance, tossing graceful arcs of line out toward the concentric swirls of hungry fish. Up ahead, Tasha's bear bells played a jingle as she romped up and down the valley floor. She was happy to be free at last after 2,000 miles of blacktop, strange-smelling rest stops, and incomprehensible books-on-tape.

Cresting the rocky flanks of Lonesome Mountain above Albino Lake, we came to two large lakes connected by 300 yards of fast-moving riffles. Even in August, the upper lake, Jasper, was almost completely encircled with snow, while the lower lake, Golden, was rimmed with steep snowfields tinged a startlingly bright red from dying algae. Halfway between the lakes, on a grassy bench tucked away out of the wind behind huge boulders, was a perfect tent site. We quickly set up camp and then headed to the stream to check out the prospects.

Dan, the savviest angler in the group, put on a drab green army-surplus jacket and crawled the last few yards through the grass to the side of the stream. After a few moments of peering over the rim through his polarized glasses, he motioned that there were several large cutthroat finning in the eddies. Ever so stealthily, he eased the tip of his rod over the eddy, suspended the fly in front of the fish, and, using an arcane technique called dapping, teased the fish into striking. It was fly-fishing as practiced in the Middle Ages, before the advent of fancy reels and floating line. Before long, Dan had a pair of eighteen-inch cuts flopping in the grass as he coached us in the covert art of stalking spawning trout.

That was several days and many fish ago. Tonight, as the stars reel overhead and the fire's last embers pulse and glow, I linger awhile before turning in. I'm just glad to be here—pack off, feet up—surrounded by intoxicating beauty. The map shows some lakes high up on the plateau, way up among the ripsaw summits and the blue glacier tongues. There are fish up in those lakes, big fish. That's where we'll head tomorrow.

The setting sun ignites a bank of clouds above Paradise Valley in Montana.

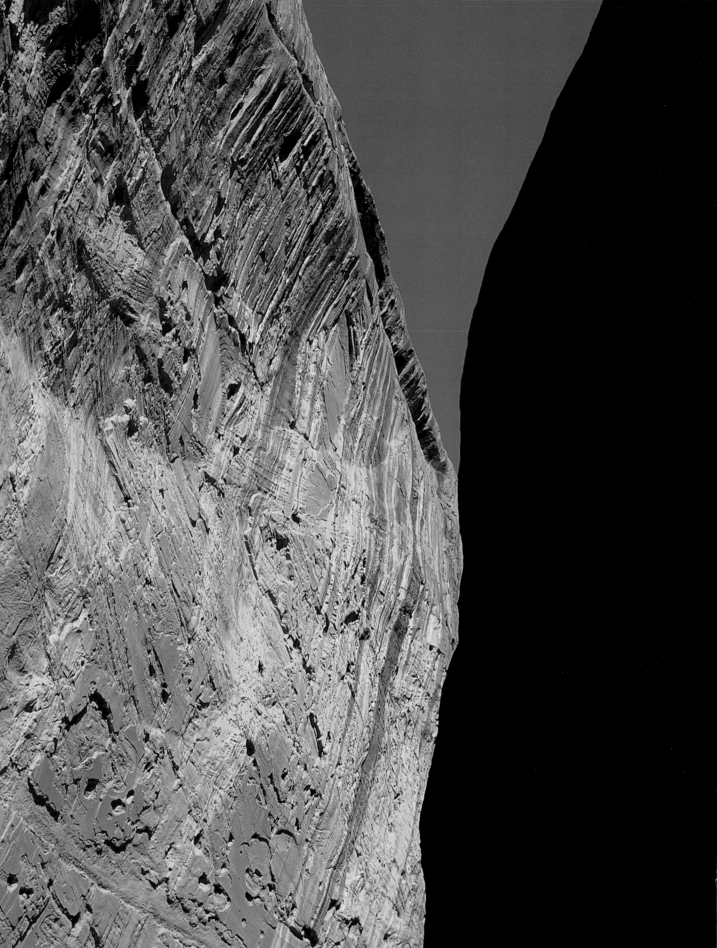

HOODOOS
AND
SLICKROCK

Escalante National Monument, Utah

A VAST EMPTY SWEEP of red rock and blue sky stretches from the Grand Staircase country in the west, scrambles over the wild arid heights of the Kaiparowits Plateau, then tumbles eastward down to the twisted slick-rock folds of the Escalante River. This is a pristine and little-known collection of badlands, broken cliffs, and mazelike canyons. And though it is a severe country, rough and jumbled, its awesome ruggedness possesses an almost ethereal beauty.

This land of wind and space, of solitude and distance, is the Grand Staircase–Escalante National Monument—1.7 million acres deep in the blood-red, rocky heart of southern Utah's canyon country. In the far distance, etched against the heavens, turrets and spires, domes and pinnacles, arches and weathered multicolored cliffs rise into air so clean and dry that gazing about is like looking through a magnifying glass. Closer, a collection of hoodoo rocks, a gang of hobgoblins, march past in stony silence. Caprocks sprout like giant red toadstools from the sandstone.

Light and shadows create a perfect contrast deep in the recesses of Little Death Hollow.

Edward Abbey called this country home. It's a piece of the planet the desert anarchist and defender of wild places considered "the center of the world, God's navel, the red wasteland." Ever since I read *Desert Solitaire*, Abbey's classic account of the seasons he spent as a ranger at Arches National Monument, I have longed to explore this American Eden. Now, twenty years later, I'm following Cactus Ed's tracks across the slickrock.

Abbey loved rattling off his favorite place names: Deadhorse Point, Hells Backbone, Robbers Roost. Names on the land are a poetry of place, and here they speak to the tough, unforgiving nature of the Grand Staircase–Escalante: Little Death Hollow, Carcass Canyon, Spooky Gulch. This is a feral wilderness, a place to lose oneself in fragile splendor and raw freedom.

One who did lose himself in the tortured labyrinths of the Escalante country was Everett Ruess, a young artist, writer, and solitary traveler who

---

Rambling across the sagebrush flats of Fiftymile Bench, the Explorer follows the rough trail beneath the bony cliffs of the Kaiparowits Plateau.

found the siren song of the desert southwest irresistible. "I have loved the red rocks, the twisted trees, the red sand blowing in the wind, the slow, sunny clouds crossing the sky, the shafts of moonlight on my bed at night," he wrote. "I have seemed to be at one with the world." Ruess was last seen alive by a pair of sheepherders in the canyons of the Escalante in 1934. He was just twenty years old when he disappeared, and his body has never been found.

Adventure is what Dan Berns and I expect to find here, knowing full well that adventure can quickly turn to disaster in this fierce and dangerous land. The dangers are real and many: flash floods, dehydration, quicksand, and violent weather are just a few of the potential hazards. The monument is remote, just about as far out there as you can get in the lower forty-eight, and its roads and trails are few, primitive, and not well-maintained. Out here we are pretty much on our own.

That, of course, is Escalante's allure.

CALF CREEK FALLS

The trail climbs alongside a clear, cold creek flowing out of a steep-sided canyon. On either side, reddish walls of Navaho sandstone streaked with

black stripes of desert varnish rise to block the sky; we peer upward in wonder at the sheer rock walls aflame in the rich red afternoon light.

Grand Staircase–Escalante National Monument is a big place, more off-the-beaten-path than most. Pulling in to the little hamlet of Escalante, we stopped to check the map. Four-wheel-drive tracks and nameless trails led off in all directions. But one path, the trail to Calf Creek Falls, was just ahead, a roughly six-mile round-trip featuring a 126-foot waterfall—just the thing to get us out of the truck and onto the land. If we hustled, we would be back by dark.

Now, still within a hundred yards of the trailhead, we look up to the left and see a perfect miniature arch carved in the sandstone by wind and water. The opening is a mere two feet in diameter, but I know it took the elements thousands of years to fashion that small round opening. The workmanship is exquisite. Stopping to look at the arch, I take a deep breath and feel the stress of travel seep away. I look around at the juniper, the pinyon pine scarred by a hungry porcupine searching for the tender inner bark, and I realize with a sense of relief that I am finally here.

The trail leads through saltbush and rabbitbrush. Most of the deciduous trees—the Gambel oaks, the box elders—have lost their leaves to the

A collection of hoodoo rocks—a gang of hobgoblins—marches past in stony silence.

—

91

advancing season, but the prickly pear cactus are doing fine. Their flat, spiny stems line the path, and we watch where we put our feet. Soon we pass the remains of an old fence. Long ago, some rancher realized that if he put this barrier here to keep his calves from wandering downstream, the impassable sandstone walls on either side and at the head of the canyon would do the rest. Over time this perfect natural pasture became known as Calf Creek Canyon.

The calves are long gone, but the beavers have been hard at work here, building dams across the creek and forming ponds and marshes. As we hike past, flocks of mallards explode from the water in a hurry to get out of range, this being hunting season. The creek itself is filled with trout; where the trail passes near the stream we see dozens of the fish finning lazily above the shallow sandy bottom.

"Look up there." Dan points across the canyon. The sandstone wall opposite us is lit up as if by stage lights, made more dramatic by the brood-

ing dark sky above. I look closely and then I see a window in the stone halfway up the opposite cliff. The window is almost completely walled up with red brick, clearly the work of a stonemason. It's a thousand-year-old granary where the Indians who lived in this canyon and farmed its fertile bottom stored their harvest.

I am imagining who lived here and what their lives were like when Dan and I see something even more extraordinary across the river. There, on a smooth wall of sandstone in a deeply recessed alcove, we see three very large humanlike figures painted in red. The figures stand three abreast and appear to be holding hands. Who are they? Gods? Heroes? Or is it the representation of some ceremony or event in the life of the artist?

The light is fading. Now only the very top of the rimrock is still lit by the occasional ray of light slipping through a crack in the clouds. Another mile up the trail and we feel a cool breeze soughing down canyon and we put on fleece jackets. Soon we reach trail's end.

Far beyond to the north and east, the snowcapped Henry Mountains rise above the red canyon country like a bank of snowy clouds.

—

93

At the head of the canyon, a stream of silvery water pours over a lip of rock 126 feet above. The water free-falls and crashes on the sloping canyon wall before sliding into the deep green pool below. A cool mist fills the evening air, trapped inside this perfect grotto by the parabolic rock walls that reach hundreds of feet into the starry sky.

With a half-moon rising, we follow the sandy white trail back through the darkness. Off to the right, something rustles the dry autumn leaves and then moves away, up a side canyon into the night.

BATTLEGROUND

Further investigation reveals a pictograph mural. We trade gazes with several otherworldly figures, painted by human hands 1,000 years ago.

"So, how did *you* find out about this place?" The question sounds like a challenge. I'm not quite sure how to respond. I toss on my pack, pat my pockets to make sure I have the key, then slam the truck door.

"Oh, it's been in the news a lot lately, I guess."

My interrogator replies with a disgusted shake of his head. He is a young man in his late twenties. We've never met before, and he isn't exactly being friendly. He is carrying a hard-used backpack and looks trail-worn. There's a coating of red dust on his clothing, his boots are caked with red mud.

Soon his hiking partner appears from around the corner of the trail. They drop their packs with a heavy thud in the red dust at the trailhead and take long, thirsty drinks from their water bottles.

"I've been coming here for years," says the second hiker after a moment. "And it's not the same anymore. Ever since this place was made into a national monument, all the magazines, all the newspapers have been carrying stories telling folks to come out here. People from New York and California. Before you know it, this area is going to be overrun."

Dan and I trade looks. An unspoken message passes between us: "It's probably not a good idea to mention the cameras and notepads in our backpacks. These guys probably don't want to hear that we're going to tell the world about their favorite canyon."

I can't say I blame them. Ever since President Clinton set aside the Grand Staircase–Escalante National Monument in 1996, earnest people who care about wild country have argued over whether or not official designation for these canyons and cliffs in southern Utah is a good thing. These hikers clearly feel national monument status will be the ruin of the Escalante country. And they aren't alone.

What these hikers fear is the plague Edward Abbey called "industrial tourism." When Abbey coined the term, he was lamenting the transformation of the obscure little national monument where he was a seasonal ranger, Arches, into a full-fledged automobile-accessible national park. Like these two backcountry ramblers just in from the canyons of the Escalante, Abbey was happiest poking around his 33,000-acre backyard by himself, sharing it with the deer, mountain lions, black widow spiders, and scorpions. When pavement, parking lots, and visitor facilities finally came to Arches, the wilderness qualities that made the place unique were eradicated. As he laments in *Desert Solitaire*, "It is an old story in the Park Service."

At the trail register I sign in, then read the comments written there by my fellow hikers. The record is a battle of words concerning the future of Escalante, and the register captures the feelings on both sides of the issue:

"Keep the National Park Service out!"

"Long live the government."

Dan and I start down the dry, sandy streambed of Hurricane Wash. We're headed to Coyote Gulch, a side canyon with a clear, quick tributary flowing into the Escalante River. Hurricane Wash flows across a boulder plain for several miles, then starts narrowing as it carves through the red rock, dropping deeper into the earth with each passing mile. In places where red clay banks line the wash we see the delicate heart-shaped tracks of deer. The wind has worn a thin, elegant sandstone arch into the top of a red rock dome.

Tonight, camped on a bench above the stream, safe from the flash floods that scour these canyons clean, I lean back in my camp chair and watch as the moon crests the canyon rim. The silence, the solitude, is complete. Later, heading for my sleeping bag, I think about what those two hikers wrote in the trail register:

"Stop Industrial Tourism!"

OVERLEAF:
This is a pristine and little-known land of rugged badlands, broken cliffs, and mazelike canyons. And though it is a severe country, rough and jumbled, its awesome ruggedness possesses an almost ethereal beauty.

COYOTE GULCH

We're out of our sleeping bags before first light, sipping coffee as the stars fade from the night sky. From my perch on the sandstone slab I glance over at Dan, who is looking more like a desert rat every day. And then I remember the quandary we've put ourselves in by just being here, by being emissaries from the world beyond the canyon rim. Brooding, I gaze at the silent stone, at the prickly pear cactus, at the trickle of water running between the parallel sandstone walls. Those hikers were right, I decide. And somebody has got to take a stand.

Just look at Dan, I think. A refugee from modern times. The canyon has cast a magic spell over him. He looks relaxed, content, at peace. What kind of sanctuary will this canyon offer if it is overrun with pilgrims like us seeking respite from a world gone mad? Where will people go to re-create themselves?

I'm filled with resolve. Just this once, I'm going to do the right thing. I tell Dan to forget the cameras, forget the tripod, forget all this high technology. Toss it all down a slot in the rock somewhere where no one will ever find it. Leave the canyon be, I urge him. Don't tell a soul what we've found down here.

Dan takes a philosophical sip of coffee.

"And then you'll be fired," he says amiably.

I think about that for a moment.

"Let's go," I say.

Once again we toss on our packs and enter the narrowing defile. As we hike, the walls get gradually higher and steeper until they loom hundreds of feet above our heads. For some reason the trees down here in the belly of the earth are still resplendent in fall colors though most of the foliage has faded from the trees up on the plain above. The bright yellows and golds are a pleasing complement to the infinite shades of canyon red.

After a mile of easy hiking, we come to the junction with Coyote Gulch. This stream is wider and more voluminous than Hurricane Wash, and from here on we jump or wade the stream at every bend. The canyon begins to twist and turn in a serpentine course toward its meeting with the Escalante River, some eight looping miles downstream.

We come to a great bend in the river, where the waters of ten million flash floods have carved an enormous overhang in the canyon wall. At the

deepest part of the bend, the rim forms a sweeping roof perhaps 100 feet above our heads, a roof that hangs a good 100 feet out over the river. It's like looking out from inside a massive cave. The acoustics are fantastic, and the echo takes almost a full second to return.

"WHO ARE YOU?" shouts Dan.

"WHO ARE YOU?" replies the canyon.

Another turn and we come face to face with Lobo Arch. According to Rudi Lambrechtse's *Hiking the Escalante*, though this arch is now called Jacob Hamblin Arch, the original settlers called it Lobo, after a legendary wolf that developed an unfortunate taste for cattle. The wolf's career finally ended when a hunter lured him into a trap and shot him, but not before the lobo dragged that trap for ten miles. We agree with Rudi. Lobo it is.

Another turn, another giant overhang, another fantastic rock formation. This one is called Coyote Natural Bridge, and it is a beautiful portal framing the entrance to the lower canyon. After a few miles of stream-jumping and

Another turn, another giant overhang, another fantastic rock formation. This one is called Coyote Natural Bridge, and it is a lovely portal framing the entrance to the lower canyon.

The walls of the canyon are perfectly smooth, almost as if sanded and buffed to a slick shiny surface.

foot-slogging, we come to a wide, grassy valley. A game trail ascends the slope to our left, up to a terrace recessed under an overhang in the cliff. We decide it will do nicely for a lunch spot and begin the long hike up.

At the crest it is quite clear that others have had the same idea. There is charcoal scattered about, and bones, and bits of flint. There is a stone enclosure, with walls made of ochre rock held together by mortar. I can see the imprints of the mason's fingers between the stones. Inside the enclosure, more charcoal, more bone, and several corncobs. We've stumbled into an ancient cliff dwelling. Further investigation reveals a pictograph mural. We eat our peanut butter sandwiches under the watchful gaze of several otherworldly figures, painted by human hands some 1,000 years ago.

SPOOKY CANYON

A narrow dirt track studded with boulders and riven by deep gullies and tooth-jarring washboards traverses a vast, empty sweep of Utah desert. From behind the wheel I see a world of sagebrush, red rock, and blue sky stretching from the bony cliffs of the Kaiparowits Plateau to the serpentine chasms of the Escalante River.

At the crest we find a stone enclosure made with walls of red rock held together by mortar. We've stumbled into an ancient cliff dwelling.

Rambling across the sagebrush flats of Fiftymile Bench, the Ford Explorer follows the rough road, bouncing toward the ever-receding horizon. Suddenly, from up near the right front tire, a big black-tailed jackrabbit bursts from cover. He bounds away in a panic, conquering distance with impressive twenty-foot leaps, leaving us literally in his dust as I slow to cross a washout where a flash flood took a huge bite of road as it roared by to join the river miles away.

The gully is deep and sports an impressive set of sharp, oil-pan-ripping stones lying in wait for the unwary. For perhaps the tenth time this morning, Dan jumps out of the passenger seat to do a little road work. Pushing and shoving, he removes the snaggletoothed rocks. After he clears the path I depress the accelerator ever so slightly, trying to gain purchase without spinning the wheels. Instead, I send a shotgun blast of sand and gravel flying back as the vehicle lurches out of the ravine. Fortunately, Dan had the good sense to stand off to the side.

"Well," he says as he gets back in, "I guess the sign wasn't kidding."

The sign, which we had seen impaled in the red earth some miles back, simply said, "CAUTION: FOUR WHEEL DRIVE ONLY." I had supposed it meant that the path ahead was ungraded, unpaved, primitive—in short, unfit for most vehicle travel. Perfect. It might as well have said "FUN AHEAD." We rocked and rolled right past it with anticipation of good things to come.

Continuing on toward the next obstacle, I remind Dan what Edward Abbey said about off-road driving: "A four-wheel-drive trail may be defined as any pair of wheel tracks which gets you into trouble, creates demoralizing repair bills, and generally goes nowhere."

"Well, that settles it," says Dan. "Nothing to do but plunge ahead."

Perhaps as an afterthought, another sign a little farther on says, "WARNING: ROADS MAY BECOME IMPASSABLE WHEN WET." Accustomed to a bedrock substrate of hard New Hampshire granite, I have no idea what this sign is talking about, so I promptly forget all about it.

The significance of the second message becomes clear the next morning when a heavy bank of gray cloud settles in and proceeds to drop a nasty mixture of snow, sleet, and freezing rain on our heads, turning the red clay surface of the Jeep track into a thick, sticky, viscous bouillabaisse the locals call gumbo. This Cajun-sounding stuff is so tenacious it clings like plaster, and before long our hiking boots weigh about ten pounds apiece. With relief we break camp, toss the gear in the back of the truck, and get ready to ride.

Reefs and boulders of red rock are etched against a sky so clear it is like looking through a magnifying glass.

It's obvious even to us that we risk getting stuck, but we take up the challenge. We've got our camping gear, extra gas, and ample food and water. If we get stuck, who cares? Undaunted, we forge ahead. All goes well for about fifty yards. Then the Explorer skids crazily, as if on glare ice.

Steering madly, Dan somehow manages to keep the vehicle between the ditches. When we glide to a ludicrous halt facing 180 degrees from our earlier direction of travel, I get out to see what just happened. The tire lugs are packed solid with gumbo, making them as bald as a Marine recruit, offering zero traction. Admitting defeat, we slip and slide the vehicle back to camp, where we ignominiously clomp around in our absurd mud boots and pray for a change in the weather.

We don't have to wait long. In the evening as the sun drops behind the Straight Cliffs, a high-pressure system comes knifing down from the north, dropping the temperature and sweeping the skies clean. Tomorrow the road will be dry. We set up the tent on the slickrock amidst domes and pinnacles of wind-worn sandstone. Chilly, we don our down jackets and build a crackling fire of pinion and juniper, then relax in our camp chairs and watch the bright sparks drift from the licking flames upward toward the icy stars.

The sign simply said: "Caution: Four Wheel Drive Only." We rocked and rolled right past it with anticipation of good things to come.

Strangely, I'm elated to be stuck. There are so few places left where nature still calls the shots. Even with our burly vehicle, we're shut down until further notice, and that's that. Things could be worse. The hunter, Orion, flies through the deep indigo night, returning our gaze from above. Coyotes yip and howl like lunatics from somewhere in the sagebrush beyond the dancing circle of light. My last thought before curling up in my sleeping bag is that I'm in a magical place, far beyond all that is safe, comfortable, familiar, and dull. I am exactly where I want to be. It's a big, raw, awesomely beautiful world out here, and there's not another human being within fifty miles.

In the morning we're free to go. We mount up the Explorer and hit the trail.

Dan grinds to a halt at the edge of a precipice. Trail's end. Lunch, water, and extra layers go into the daypacks. Ahead of us is a steep sandstone escarpment dropping off perhaps 100 feet into a sandy dry wash. Beyond, as far as we can see, is an endless country of creases and folds that looks like an unmade bed after a night of really bad dreams. Somewhere down there in those tangled sheets of stone is, appropriately enough, Spooky Canyon, our destination for today.

We drop off the lip into the gulch below, and whatever features were

The Henry Mountains rise 5,000 feet above the surrounding red-rock plateau. The range is so remote, the first recorded sighting was by members of John Wesley Powell's Colorado River expedition in 1869.

visible from above are lost in the maze. I wonder if we could even find our way back to the Explorer. It occurs to me to check the map.

"Hey, where's the map?"

"I thought you had it."

So it goes. Map recovered, compasses oriented, we follow Coyote Dry Fork until we spill out onto a broad, sandy outwash plain. Looking up to our left we see a tunnel of red sandstone boring down from who-knows-where. The insides of the tunnel are perfectly smooth, almost as if sanded and buffed to a slick shiny surface.

"That's it," says Dan. "Peek-A-Boo Canyon. Let's go."

Entering the canyon is not as easy as it appears. The rock is so smooth it takes us several attempts to ascend the first pour-over. Then the fun begins.

The first thing we see is a perfect double arch spanning the roof of the narrowing canyon. We climb through the spans and suddenly the walls constrict to a width of about two feet. The sky is completely shut off, and as the canyon corkscrews through the rock, our visibility is limited to only a foot or two in either direction. Just enough light filters down through the crack of roof somewhere far above to cast an ethereal, rose-tinted glow. Our voices don't exactly echo in here, they resonate as though we were speaking through organ pipes.

Chilly, we build a crackling fire of pinion and juniper, then relax and watch the bright sparks drift from the licking flames up toward the icy stars.

The swirly rock tunnel climbs gradually, and like moles we burrow until we emerge back onto the slickrock bench at the top of the canyon.

"This is unbelievable."

"Wait 'till you see this."

"Hold on. Let's take a picture. Where are you?"

"Right next to you, around the corner. Here's the camera."

Every now and then the narrow slot is jammed by chockstones, boulders that were swept into the tight crevasse by flash floods. These we surmount by bracing our hands and feet against the opposite sides of the slot and "chimneying" straight up and over the obstructions. Some chockstones are wedged ten or twenty feet above us, and these we merely slip beneath.

"You know how those rocks got jammed up there, don't you?" asks Dan from beneath one tightly wedged boulder.

"Yeah, flash floods. You wouldn't have much of a chance if you got caught in here," I reply.

Like moles we burrow upward until we emerge back onto the slickrock bench at the top of the canyon. Suddenly, the world above-ground seems inexpressibly vast.

Next up is Spooky, and we head cross-country, keeping a close eye on the map and terrain as we navigate the half mile or so to the next canyon. It may be a rather unscientific description, but Spooky is like a funhouse at an amusement park. The canyon starts tight and gets tighter, until we are slipping sideways through the slot, in some places holding our breath to slither through. Sometimes the slot tilts forwards or backwards, and we find ourselves practically wedged on our backs or on our chests as we squirm through the cracks.

"Not a place for a claustrophobe," I hear Dan say from somewhere up ahead.

Like true subterraneans, we finally emerge from Spooky at dusk. There's one more slot canyon, Brimstone, nearby. I suggest we try it.

"Isn't Brimstone where that guy got stuck for eight days and almost died?" Dan asks.

As casually as possible, I look west toward the setting sun. "It's getting kind of late." I shrug. "Let's save Brimstone for another trip."

HOLE-IN-THE-ROCK

Crystalline days flow by, each one more gorgeous than the last. We hike the canyons, scramble up to ancient cliff dwellings, ponder the meaning of mysterious Anasazi pictographs, and tramp the rimrock of the Circle Cliffs in the burnished light of dawn. As the end of our time in Escalante draws near, there is one last place we want to see: the Hole-in-the-Rock, where one of the most audacious feats in the history of the American West took place.

In the autumn of 1879, the Mormon Church organized an expedition to settle the wild lands around the San Juan River in southeastern Utah. Some 250 men, women, and children responded to the call, and in one of the great pioneering epics of the American West, they made the long and dangerous trip from Escalante to what is now Bluff, Utah.

The pioneers packed everything they would need to build their new homes—garden seeds, farm tools and implements, 200 horses, and more than 1,000 head of cattle. Then, dismissing more lengthy routes to the north and south, they headed in a straight line toward their destination, not knowing what lay ahead but confident they could overcome any obstacle. Their worries about their ability to traverse the rugged country ahead were tempered by faith that they were on a divine mission.

The road-building went smoothly for the first fifty miles, but as the party approached the Colorado River, advance scouts brought back troublesome news. There was no good route down into the depths of Glen Canyon and across the roiling river. As the wagons crept across the final six miles of tortured slickrock to the edge of the sheer precipice, the future of the expedition was in serious doubt.

The route looked impossible. Two thousand feet below, the Colorado blocked their path. Undaunted, the expedition engineers chose a cleft in the canyon rim called Hole-in-the-Rock as the spot to descend. Crews were dispatched with picks and blasting powder, and a dangerously steep, crude

OVERLEAF:
Escalante is at
the heart of a
wealth of public
lands, including
Bryce Canyon
National Park,
where ranks of
hoodoos and hob-
goblins march
through time in
perfect formation.

wagon road was blasted out of stone. In places, steps were carved into the sandstone. The wagons were lowered, and six weeks later the entire expedition had made the descent, ferried the river, and climbed out of the canyon on the opposite side.

The road they built became known as the Hole-in-the-Rock Road, and it was never used again. Today, the ruts across the sagebrush plain left by their eighty wagons are still visible. A modern Jeep trail roughly parallels the Mormon route, and a journey down the Hole-in-the-Rock Road is still an adventure, as Dan and I discover.

The first fifty miles of the road go smoothly for us as well. The ruts and washes we cross every so often pose no challenge for the Explorer, and the miles fly by.

When we approach the Hole-in-the-Rock, still some six miles distant, the route becomes difficult. Gone is the sandy, washboarded path through the sage.

Ahead is only rock, in places deeply gouged by erosion, in others scarred with steep gullies and ravines just inches to the left or right of our tires. Frequently we stop, scout out a route, and cautiously move ahead.

We take turns at the wheel, creeping along in low gear, inching across the cross-bedded sandstone, the petrified dunes of the Navajo formation. Like the Mormon pioneers, we build a road in places by filling gaps with boulders, by building rock bridges across spans that would bottom-out the vehicle, and simply by moving rocks out of the way. Picking our way through the shock-busting chuckholes and axle-breaking washouts, we gain appreciation for what those hardy pioneers achieved.

Slowly, we pass under the massive red bulk of the Kaiparowits Plateau, which rises high above us like the prow of a mighty ship. The sun strikes hammer blows from a perfect sky, and the heat bounces off the white rock below. There isn't a sound save for the slow crunching of the tires or the sigh of the warm breeze swirling across the smooth rock face. Finally, there's a notch like a gunsight in the canyon rim. Hole-in-the-Rock. We get out and climb through the gap, down to the sparkling blue waters of Lake Powell, following the pioneers down stairs hand-hewn from the rock more than a century ago.

Back on top, we stop for a moment to catch our breath and look out over this land that we have come to know well. To the west, terraced Kaiparowits looms large in the warm dry air. To the north lie the twisted canyons of the Escalante River. Far beyond to the north and east, the snow-capped Henry Mountains rise above the red canyon country like a bank of snowy clouds.

There it is, I think. There's your monument.

But what makes this place so special? I wonder. The geologic formations are spectacular, to be sure, but no more so than those in other places throughout the Southwest. In fact, nearby Bryce and Zion National Parks have more sensational scenery. Is it the ancient Indian sites? No, the sites here are not really all that remarkable, compared to Mesa Verde, or Chaco Canyon, or a dozen other places where ancient cities still stand. Is it the history? Certainly there are fascinating tales in this landscape, particularly the story of this rough-hewn road I'm standing on, but no more than many historic regions throughout the Southwest.

No, what makes the Escalante so special isn't the geology, or the prehistory, or the history. What make it special is that it's big and undeveloped, roomy enough and wild enough to get lost in, to have adventures in. When people say in the visitor registers "Don't change a thing!" they are saying, "Let this remain a place where we can set out on our own and discover things for ourselves. Let us get lost if we misread the map. Let us get stuck if we find ourselves at the bottom of a Jeep trail in a downpour. Let us have adventures, too."

Dan and I get back in the truck. Tomorrow we're hiking to Little Death Hollow and through Wolverine Canyon. We'll be out there for several days, we're not sure how many. The locals say it's a quite a trip, if you don't mind humping a heavy pack through miles and miles of blasted, eroded, twisted, and contorted red-rock wasteland.

We don't mind. That's what we came for.

The bright yellows and golds of autumn leaves are a pleasing complement to the infinite shades of canyon red.

DESERT
INFERNO

Death Valley National Park, California

I T ' S M I D N I G H T I N G L I T T E R G U L C H . Crowds swarm toward dazzling casinos where the drinks are free, the food all-you-can-eat, and most of the patrons will have their pockets picked clean by their smiling hosts after a few hours at the tables and slots.

Back in the shadows, like a couple of trail-worn misfits in a road movie or members of some strange millennialist cult, Dan Berns and I ignore the neon come-ons and load a muddy jeep with camping supplies and gallons of water. Then, mesmerized by the surreal nature of it all, we cruise the strip, find our way out past the sprawling suburbs, and head west from Las Vegas into the high desert night. Looking back I can see the Sahara, Dunes, and Mirage pulsing in the rearview mirror.

Beyond the bouncing headlights and an endless stream of tractor-trailer trucks, the Mojave Desert stretches off in eerie desolation. Around two o'clock in the morning, we pull off the highway into the tiny desert oasis of Baker, California, where we admire the world's tallest thermometer, a towering instrument that records 120 degrees Fahrenheit with menacing regularity. Then, buzzing with road-weariness (we had started the day camped along the Paria River in southern Utah), we tap our energy reserves and take off down a rugged jeep track, wrestling the wheel in the general direction of a place called the Devil's Playground.

For another hour we jackhammer across dry washes and ancient lava flows, past the cinder cones of extinct volcanoes and the grim bones of ill-fated creatures. Finally, cresting a hill, we grind to a halt. Dead tired, heads

Dan Berns hikes into the heart of Death Valley. Somewhere out here in the blinding crust is the lowest spot in the western hemisphere: 282 feet below sea level.

pounding with fatigue, we get out of the vehicle and sway groggily under a moonless sky full of van Gogh stars swirling in the clear desert night. With hardly a word we put up the tent, crawl in our bags, and go to sleep. Just before nodding off, I happen to look up through the mosquito netting and I awake with a start. There's a grotesque, shadowy figure looming right outside the tent. Alarmed, with visions of homicidal survivalists and random desert oddballs flashing through my addled brain, I bolt upright.

And then I see it's a Joshua tree. Like the Old Testament prophet who raised his arms to God, the bizarre tree's weirdly human limbs sweep upward in pious supplication to heaven. I let out a deep breath, lie back, and shut my eyes. I don't rouse until the big red sun crests the blasted hills to the east. And though it's autumn, the cool season in the desert, by the time I get out of my sleeping bag the tent is roasting like an oven.

When we set out from Las Vegas, we had only a vague idea of where we were heading. In the best American tradition of the open road, we had a vehicle at our disposal, a continent to explore, and just enough time to get really, truly lost. The one sure thing we knew was that, with admirable foresight, Congress had acted to preserve one of the most diverse desert environments in the world when in 1994 it passed the California Desert Protection Act. The Act set aside some 9.2 million acres—an area roughly equivalent to Massachusetts, Connecticut, and Rhode Island combined.

We are somewhere in the northern part of the new Mojave National Preserve, a 1.6 million-acre stretch of some of the most extreme, some would say godforsaken, country on earth. As we eat our breakfast, we study the map spread out over the jeep's hood. To the south lies Joshua Tree National Park and its fantastic collection of red-rock formations. To the north, Death Valley—the largest National Park in the lower forty-eight states. Unable to decide, I turn to the guidebook for inspiration. It flips open to Death Valley, and I read:

"As its name suggests, Death Valley is an inhuman environment: barren and monotonous, burning hot and almost entirely without shade, much less water. At first sight it seems impossible that the landscape could support life of any kind. . . ."

"Sounds like a challenge," says Dan through a mouthful of cereal.

And so we go. North of Baker, we enter a region of towering white sand dunes like those straight out of *Lawrence of Arabia*. We pull off the road and follow a little jeep track toward the graceful piles swooping hundreds of feet into the deep blue sky. Not far from their base we are surprised to find a clear stream racing across the desert floor. The chuckling water is refreshingly cool, and in that paradoxical situation we take a delightful dip and wash away three days worth of road grime and desert dust. To dry off we merely stand and let the moisture evaporate.

Back on the main road Dan suddenly exclaims, "Stop. Did you see that? It looked like a big brown glove skittering across the road."

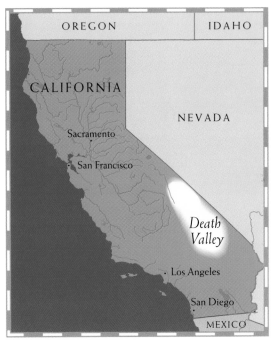

We back up, get out, and meet our first tarantula, a hairy, many-legged fellow about the size of, well, a big brown glove.

Cresting Jubilee Pass in the crusty Black Mountains, we begin our descent into Death Valley. The landscape stretching out before us is appalling, like a giant construction site. Everywhere, countless tons of mud, sand, and rocks deposited by flash floods tearing down from the mountains spread out like brown glaciers in immense alluvial fans. A few scraggly mesquite trees provide a faint tint of green in a land that Edward Abbey, that misanthropic old desert rat, once joyously called "bitter as alkali, rough and harsh as tangled iron, miserly with life in any form." Except for the heat waves shimmering over miles of smoldering rocky debris, nothing moves. A white-hot, 200-square-mile salt pan lies at the bottom of the valley, locked in an intense staring match with the blistering sun above.

Down, down we go, past Starvation Canyon and Lost Dry Lake, Deadman Pass and Coffin Peak. Ahead, the apocalyptic mountains of the Funeral Range lean against the sky. Far beyond our line of vision, past Hells

Gate and Dry Bone Canyon, the Last Chance Range blocks all escape to the north. As the miles of scorched rubble go by, I feel we've made a terrible mistake. The country is more hostile than I had imagined.

I stop the jeep at a shallow pool seeping from the base of a cliff in the Black Mountains. The slick water spreads out across a bed of pure white table salt two miles thick. According to legend, this unlikely spring at the hottest place on earth (a temperature of 134 degrees Fahrenheit was recorded in Death Valley in 1913) was named by some forgotten prospector who tried to get his pack mule to test the water for him before he drank. The parched animal balked, so the old miner named the pool "Badwater."

There's a rumor that Badwater is poisoned with arsenic, but it isn't—a tough-as-nails species of fairy shrimp actually thrives in the salty brew. And in yet another desert paradox, Badwater's slick surface, some 279.8 feet below sea level, reflects a perfect mirror-image of snowcapped Telescope Peak, at 11,049 feet, the highest mountain in the park.

Grabbing a couple of water bottles, we hike past Badwater far out into the blistering heart of the basin. The glare off the snowy-white salt pans is brilliant, dizzying. Somewhere out here, some four miles from Badwater across the briny crust, is the lowest spot in the western hemisphere: 282 feet below sea level.

In the 1900s this town was called "The Queen City of Death Valley" and boasted a population of 10,000. By 1916 the last mine closed, and now all that remains are the silent ruins and the memories.

It's late afternoon near Furnace Creek. We spread out the map and consider evasive action. Not surprisingly, it turns out we're not the first to do so. Unknown to us, it was right here along Furnace Creek Wash in 1849 that a covered-wagon train of pioneers headed for the California goldfields strayed into what they came to call the "Valley of Death." Suffering from scurvy and starvation, the party spent nearly a month wandering across the interminable salt flats before finally escaping over a pass in the Panamints. Like our predecessors, we decide to head for the high country of the Sierra, leaving behind what one fortyniner called "the Creator's dumping ground."

We're heading for the jeep as the sun begins its long descent behind the lofty peaks of the Panamint Range. And then I notice that the rugged

Death Valley can be a cruel, unforgiving place, but as we gain altitude the air cools considerably. We brush through green clumps of juniper, and higher still, the trail enters a stand of pinyon pine.

Barrel cactus and an abandoned miner's wheelbarrow grace a sun-blasted hillside in the Funeral Range.

hills and barren mountains have blossomed into an artist's palette of colors. The landscape pulses with splendid golden light so rich the very rock seems to glow from within. Everywhere we look, the land is daubed with stunning bands of deep red, pink, yellow, orange, green, and turquoise.

I fold the map and stare. The air is so clear and the long, rich beams of sunlight so distilled, the texture of the rock and the delicate shades of color are revealed in startling and exquisite detail. We grab our day-packs and wander for miles up a twisting golden canyon until the sunlight fades, the stars twinkle above, and the cool desert night settles over us. There's no longer any question of moving on. We find a campsite and put up the tent, congratulating ourselves on our wise decision to spend time here in this eccentric, forbidding, yet seductive wilderness.

Two days later we lurch the vehicle into a corkscrew canyon deep in the Panamint Range not far, as it turns out, from where Charles Manson and his "Family" holed up in an abandoned mining camp while plotting their grisly murder spree. The jeep track ends abruptly at a cavernous

washout where we encounter a hermit named "Jim" living in a beat-up old trailer resting in the shade of a couple of date palms.

Shirtless, clad in an ancient pair of filthy brown corduroys and wiping his hands with a greasy cloth, Jim emerges from a corrugated-tin shed. For a couple of bucks he offers to keep an eye on the jeep for us.

"Say, you fellas don't happen to have any tobacco, do you?" he asks. "I ain't been to town since before I don't know when."

Lean and wiry, with graying black hair, a gap-toothed smile, and leathery skin, Jim lives on the hidden edge of the park like an old-time pickax and pack-mule prospector. Except he's not a character out of a novel or a history book. He's flesh and bone, kin to men like Shorty Borden, a Death Valley loner who in 1932 built a nine-mile road by hand to his silver and lead diggings up Hanaupau Canyon.

Day after day, month after month, Shorty picked and pried under the broiling sun, in the end only to discover it would cost him more to transport the ore to a smelter than the ore was worth. Oh well. Shorty's epitaph,

This unlikely spring at the hottest place on earth was named "Badwater" by a prospector whose thirsty mule refused to drink the salty brine.

which he composed himself, sums up his life. It reads: "Here lies Shorty Harris, a single blanket jackass prospector."

When he died, Shorty was buried next to his pal Jim Dayton, another old desert rat who was literally killed by the heat in 1899. According to legend, when Dayton's body was found stretched out under the negligible shade of a mesquite tree, his wagon barrels were still full of water. Sadly, his mules couldn't get to it. The helpless creatures died of thirst still strapped in their harnesses.

Death Valley can be a cruel, unforgiving place, but as we hike up the canyon we enter a different world. The trail follows a clear, cold mountain stream cascading over rocks and ledges and plunges into deep pools and potholes. Scarlet tufts of Indian paintbrush line the path, while bouquets of rare, buttery Panamint daisies sway in the cool breeze flowing down-

The air is so clear, and the long, rich beams of sunlight so distilled, the texture of the rock and the delicate shades of color are revealed in startling and exquisite detail.

canyon. Here and there, hanging gardens cling to the rock walls where precious water seeps through cracks in the stone. Stout barrel cactus perch like sentries high above us on the cliff faces. Overhead, the sky is unmarred by even a single wisp of cottony cloud.

Up, up we go. As we gain altitude the air cools considerably. We jump across the stream and brush through golden willows and green clumps of juniper. Higher still, the trail enters a stand of pinyon pine, and we stop for a few minutes to gather handfuls of the ripe, delicious nuts. We see the prints and droppings of horses scattered in the pine duff. But then we realize what we're seeing isn't horse sign at all, it's the spoor of wild burros, the feral descendants of lost, abandoned, and escaped prospectors' pack animals.

The air has the cold bite of winter to it now, and we stop to put on our fleece jackets and hats. Ahead I can see snow-stuffed gullies and avalanche

paths swooping down from the highest peaks. After six miles of steady climbing, the trail levels off, widens into an old wagon road, then enters a broad valley surrounded by high timbered ridges. On both sides of the old road, dozens of stone huts and foundations line the way toward a collection of wooden buildings and a towering brick chimney rising over what appears to be a giant ore smelter.

Weary from our long hike, we trudge onward in the gathering twilight. At the center of town, wagon roads intersect, then head up toward the surrounding hillsides, climbing steep switchbacks to reach dozens of old mine adits and tailing piles.

Most of the mining debris dates back to the 1870s, when this place was known as "the toughest, rawest, most hard-boiled little hell hole that ever passed for a civilized town." In one of those bizarre twists that make the American Outback a treasure trove of stranger-than-fiction stories, this canyon was an outlaw hideout until 1873 when the outlaws themselves discovered rich veins of silver here. By 1874, the secret of the strike was out, and the outlaws-turned-miners were joined by thousands of prospectors, prostitutes, saloon keepers, gamblers, and other drifters drawn by the promise of quick riches. Frame shacks and false-front buildings sprang up under the dismal pall of the smelter smoke. Newcomers poured in daily, pitching tents or building the stone hovels by the side of the road. The canyon echoed with the ring of steel and the crack of breaking rock. Dynamite blasted the hillsides and rained tons of rubble down the slopes.

Frame shacks and false-front buildings sprang up under the dismal pall of the smelter smoke. The canyon echoed with the ring of steel and the crack of breaking rock.

The boom was over within a year, and in 1876 a flash flood roared down from the peaks and destroyed what remained of the town. Every now and then over the decades, a prospector wandered up the canyon, staying for a month, a year, to pry at the rock. As new technologies were developed, mining resumed on a sporadic basis and continued up until the late 1960s, as the sight of several abandoned pickup and two-ton trucks with bullet-shattered windshields attests. I pick up a handful of spent Smith and Wesson .38 Special cartridges scattered about in the dust at my feet.

In 1994, the canyon and the ruins were added to Death Valley National Park, and all mining officially ceased. But park or no park, as we look for a

The rugged hills and barren mountains blossomed into an artist's palette of color, washed with splendid golden light so rich the very rock seemed to glow from within.

place to pitch our tent, we see a wooden shack that looks quite occupied. We're so far out on the fringe of the park, it's quite possible some latter-day outlaw is holed up here with the ghosts. Tentatively we approach the building, mount the stairs to the porch, and knock on the door.

There's no response. I knock again. Silence. For Dan and me this feels like déjà vu. Many times over the last year we have wandered into some desolate reach of the American wilderness only to discover that it's a landscape full of surprises and unexpected encounters, a place where a step off the map brings you face-to-face with things that were supposedly lost a long, long time ago.

I turn the knob and open the door. Cold moonlight pours in through the windowpanes. As my eyes adjust to the dimness, I see two rocking chairs sitting in front of a woodstove. Split wood is stacked neatly by the back wall. The wooden floors are swept clean—there's a broom and dustpan by the door. Assorted posters are tacked on the walls, and there's a cassette player with miniature speakers sitting atop a wooden cabinet. Investigating, I find tapes in the top drawer, mostly classic American rock— Van Halen, ZZ Top, the Grateful Dead. Dan opens the kitchen cabinets. They're filled with freeze-dried and canned food, and the drawers are stocked with candles, matches, and batteries.

What have we wandered into this time? I wonder.

Dan lights a candle, then places it on the kitchen counter.

"Wait a minute, what's this?" he says, picking up a sheet of paper. In the dim candlelight it looks like a letter.

Dan reads for a moment, then laughs.

"You're not going to believe this," he says.

"What? Read it!"

"Welcome! That was quite a hike! I imagine you must be pretty tired, so take off your packs and take a seat. This is your cabin, it belongs to you. So make yourselves at home, please take care of it, and enjoy your stay." Putting the letter down, he says, "It's signed by the superintendent, Death Valley National Park."

And so we settle in. We light more candles, fashioning holders out of the tinfoil we find in the kitchen drawer. We make dinner, spread our sleeping bags on the mattresses, and build a fire in the stove to ward off the mountain chill. Late in the evening I wander outside and stand looking up at the cold stars at the dark edges of the mountains rimming the valley.

In the moonlight I can see the long-abandoned mine shafts pocking the slopes, the forlorn smelter stack stretching into the night sky, the snow gullies reaching down toward the valley floor. Shivering, I turn back to the little hut with the smoke pouring from the stovepipe, the cheery yellow light flooding from the window, the throbbing guitar strains of ZZ Top pounding through the cabin walls.

I'm heading back inside, muttering something about how bloody cold Death Valley is, when Dan puts on the Grateful Dead tape. Jerry Garcia sings, "What a long, strange trip it's been."

I couldn't agree more.

We see a wooden shack that looks quite occupied. We're so far out on the edge of the park it's quite possible some latter-day outlaw is holed up here with the ghosts.

THE
GREAT
LAND

Prince William Sound, Alaska

LAUNCHING MYSELF OFF the rail of a fishing boat, I free-fall ten feet toward the icy waters of Alaska's Prince William Sound. "This is ridiculous," I think as I splash down. The water hits my face like a blast of liquid nitrogen. I paddle over to an iceberg and haul myself out, looking like a plump red seal in my thick neoprene survival suit. From up on my icy perch I watch several other fat red seals bobbing in the frigid sea, swimming among the 'bergs several hundred yards from the base of a towering turquoise glacier. "These people are insane," I tell myself as I lie back on the ice and relax in the sunshine, hoping a hungry killer whale doesn't show now looking for a little snack.

Flanked on the west by the Kenai Mountains and on the north and east by the Chugach Range, Prince William Sound is a 15,000-square-mile arm of the Pacific Ocean jutting up into the belly of the forty-ninth state. It's a vast watery wilderness bordered by soaring snowcapped peaks sweeping down through dense northern rainforests to the sea. A maze of islands and long open reaches, the sound claims the largest collection of tidewater glaciers on the planet and is home to abundant wildlife, including whales, seals, otters, Dall sheep, mountain goats, and both black and grizzly bears.

The indomitable Captain James Cook named the sound in 1778 during a futile quest for the Northwest Passage. Though he missed the shortcut to the Orient, he discovered a region rich in natural resources, especially timber, fish, and sea otter furs. Whittier, the tiny fishing village where we began our trip, was historically a stopover for native and Russian fur traders. Miners later hiked nearby Portage Pass to reach the Iditarod Trail leading to the goldfields of Nome.

At midnight in Prince William Sound, the sea glows with the warm orange light of sunrise.

Named after the poet John Greenleaf Whittier, the modern port was built during and shortly after World War II as a military fuel storage center, and the dominant features of the town are a fuel tank farm and a giant concrete, Soviet-style high-rise apartment building where most of Whittier lives. In many ways the high-rise *is* Whittier, for it houses a store, the town hall, the post office, schools, and other municipal functions. You can live in Whittier, surrounded by some of the planet's supreme wilderness scenery, and never leave the tower. Indeed, according to local kayaker Perry Solomonson, some people never do. He knows people who have not left the building in over ten years.

A maze of islands and long open reaches, the sound claims the largest collection of tidewater glaciers on the planet.

Yesterday morning Perry, Mary, and I lashed our kayaks to the roof of *The Whittier Express*, a motor launch that shuttles kayakers into the far reaches of Prince William Sound. Outward bound in a moderate chop, the shallow draft hull slammed into each wave with a tooth-jarring concussion that made a circus act of my morning coffee ritual. Passing the mouth of Passage Canal, a deep fjord surrounded by gleaming summits riven by dozens of waterfalls cascading through the lush forests of the lower slopes in an almost tropical vision of paradise, we looked to the mountains off to the north, where a small plane had crashed in the storm the day before. There was the plane, about a thousand feet above us, clinging to the steep slope like a squashed fly on a wall. As is often the case in Alaska, nobody was hurt, and the pilot and passenger hiked back down to town.

Sometime later our captain, Pete Heddell, guided the *Express* down Culross Passage, a narrow, protected reach between Culross Island and the mainland. Pete motored right up to shore and we unloaded the kayaks in the rain. Soon, the sound of the engine was swallowed by the distance, and we were alone in the quiet, dripping wilderness. A bald eagle launched slowly from a nearby snag and flapped heavily away, weighed down by the fish in his belly. We stood quietly for a moment in the awesome silence and watched, then packed the kayaks, a tandem and a solo, and got under way.

From up on my icy perch I watch several other fat red seals bobbing in the frigid sea, swimming among the 'bergs.

It was good to be moving under our own power, to feel the familiar initial unsteadiness of the sleek narrow craft, and soon our muscles warmed to the task. In a sea kayak you sit low in the water, like a loon. Sometimes, in

We head toward a campsite on a grassy slope with commanding views up and down the fjord.

rough seas, big waves splash over the deck and you find yourself up to your armpits in the water. In a kayak you feel like a part of your surroundings, like a wild water-creature—half human, half cormorant—and less like a visitor.

Our boats glided swiftly across the aquamarine waters and the miles flew by. Rounding a point, we headed toward a waterfall cascading out of the thick wet forest. We paddled up to the foot of the falls, into a stream chock full of spawning pink salmon. We could see the fish a foot or so below us in the clear water, thrashing in the shallows. Some, totally spent, fluttered their tails weakly and languished, drifting in circles, dying. A river otter swam by with a salmon in his mouth. He was so busy with all that food we barely rated a quick glance. And then, as we sat silent and still in our kayaks, we watched a large black bear amble out of the woods just yards away. He waded into the stream and snatched a large salmon. Oblivious to us, he gripped the fish in his jaws and vanished back into the forest.

At the head of Long Bay, a rapid river full of still-vigorous, jumping salmon rushed out of the uplands. The river banks were lined with bushes heavily laden with luscious ripe salmonberries. There was enough food here to last us for weeks, an incredible display of nature's bounty in an area undisturbed by humans. We put ashore to add to our freeze-dried, store-bought fare. Perry put his rod together and quickly hooked a large male pink salmon,

called a "humpy" because of the large hump that grows on his back when he returns to his native waters to spawn. We picked berries for our cereal and took turns with the rod, catching a fish or getting a strong hit on nearly every cast.

A couple of hours later, as we threaded our way through a passage between two islands, we discovered a "pom-pom," a floating mop used to connect oil spill booms. Perry reached over the side of his kayak and retrieved it, a brightly colored souvenir of the Exxon *Valdez* oil spill.

Like many other Alaskans, Perry spent the months following the spill working feverishly to save the sound. He piloted a boat shuttling clean-up crews day and night to wherever they were needed most. "I became so exhausted," he told me, "there were times when I would literally fall asleep standing up at the wheel after dropping off a crew."

No one knew what to do when the *Valdez* sheared her hull on Bligh Reef on March 24, 1989, hemorrhaging more than 10 million gallons of North Slope crude into one of the world's most spectacular marine environments. A spill of that magnitude in such a cold and biologically rich ecosystem had never happened before.

It was the worst oil spill in U.S. history, coating hundreds of miles of pristine beaches and killing countless seabirds, salmon, otters, bears, and other animals. Paddling forward again, I brooded over our collective denial

The sun breaks out and the skies clear, revealing massive snow-draped mountains and gleaming icefields towering above a sun-splashed sea.

OVERLEAF:
The day's last rays of light strike the summits of the Kenai Mountains high above Blackstone Bay.

about what industrial development means for places like Prince William Sound. As a nation we ignored the inevitability of a major spill, preferring to believe the unthinkable couldn't happen. But when it did, rather than look inward to examine the values system that led to disaster, we pointed fingers and cast blame—at Exxon; at Alyeska, the pipeline company; at Captain Hazelwood; at everyone but ourselves. I looked around at this still recovering wilderness and wondered how we will react when the next spill happens.

The wind picked up as we approached the northern end of Culross Passage. White-caps and breakers smashed against the exposed tip of Culross Island. To continue into open water would have been foolish, so we turned around in heaving, frothy four-foot swells and beat a hasty retreat through whitecapped seas. We found a protected cove and set up camp in a heavy downpour.

To stay dry, Perry rigged up an elaborate system of waterproof tarps. Following his expert instruction, we raised tarps everywhere—tarps to cook under, tarps to relax under, and tarps over our tents to keep them dry, too. We even rigged tarps over tarps. A little later, with dry clothes, shelter, a roaring stove and a hot drink, we began to feel downright cozy. As I cooked dinner, I watched a sea otter doing the backstroke just offshore.

This morning the rain is still pouring from a leaden sky, tapping the tarps like snare drums. I get up and take a look at the water, noting the breakers crashing against the exposed shores of Culross Island across the passage from our camp. Nothing to do but wait. The others, fatalistic, retire to the tents back among the dripping spruce. But I'm anxious to move, so I sit under the tarp by the stove, sip a hot drink, and keep an eye on the wind, water, and sky.

Restless, I wander out into the rain and down through the yellow pop-weed beds to the waterline. Unlike my home waters in the Gulf of Maine, the tide here doesn't rush in and out like a raging river; it goes quietly up and down. The fjords are so deep, I realize, there are no bottom obstructions, no constraints to create flows. This part of the sound, at least, is like a

giant bathtub filled and emptied twice a day. Even though there is a twelve-foot tide, it slips in and out almost without notice.

Looking up from the shoreline to watch a bald eagle flap across the water, I notice the rain has stopped and the wind abated. The breakers across the passage are gone. I shout to the others and relieved, laughing like kids, we break camp and paddle out on glass-calm seas. Miraculously, the sun breaks out and the skies clear, revealing massive snow-draped mountains and gleaming icefields towering above a sun-splashed sea.

We set out across an expanse of sparkling blue several miles wide, aiming our bows at Blackstone Point. The warm sun feels like a massage on our cold, stiff necks and shoulders. After miles of sun-soaked kayaking, we hear the roar of powerful engines and are intercepted by a 40-foot trawler manned by Perry's friend Brad, a fisherman out of Whittier, and some of his friends. Brad offers us a lift to Blackstone Bay, a deep fjord bordered by sheer mountain walls rising out of the sea, and soon eight pairs of hands hoist our kayaks aboard.

As Brad pilots the boat across the waters of the bay, we watch a black bear gorging on berries on a steep slope a hundred feet above us. Climbing high up to the crow's nest, I can see thousands of white ice chunks carpeting the surface of the opalescent fjord.

From up here I have a startling view of the massive snout of a glacier at the end of the bay. Booming explosions rumble across the water as the great blue river of solid ice calves massive icebergs. It's a landscape still under construction, a new world in the making, and we are witnesses at the creation. I

We have a startling view of the massive snout of a glacier. It's a landscape still under construction, a new world in the making, and we are witnesses at the creation.

think of John Muir, who in the presence of the Alaskan wilderness reflected, "One easily learns that the world, though made, is yet being made."

Approaching Willard Island, Brad slows the boat and watches the depth finder, explaining that there's a bony reef reaching out from the island. We watch the little screen as it graphs the sea floor rising to meet the hull of the boat. As I wait for the grinding sound of steel hitting rock, Brad coolly inches the boat forward. The bottom rises. We move forward some more. The reef reaches for us. When we have no more room for error, the finder tracks the sea floor falling away. Soon we are breathing normally again, floating in water hundreds of feet deep.

Brad pilots the boat to the edge of the iceberg field, then makes a startling announcement. "Time for a swim," he says, passing out survival suits from the hold. A giddy mood sweeps the crew as we slip into the thick red-hooded suits, climb the rail, and leap overboard into the frigid water.

Mary is swimming on her back like a sea otter, tipping over small icebergs and joining the others in an unusual version of "King of the Hill" as they toss each other off the biggest 'berg. I can't resist. An icy splash of glacier water slaps my face as I take the plunge, but the survival suit, designed to save the lives of fishermen whose boats go down, keeps me perfectly warm. After an hour in the ice we paddle back over to the fishing boat. Brad announces that we have now been appropriately initiated to Prince William Sound, then lowers a bosun's chair and power winches each of us back up onto the deck.

The soft light of an Alaskan summer evening begins to settle over the sound, and we have about eight miles of paddling to our next camp. We lower the kayaks, get in, wave goodbye to our new friends, and paddle off.

The paddling is exquisite as we take our places in a traffic jam of icebergs floating slowly out with the tide toward the mouth of the bay. The kayaks cut swiftly through the reflected greens, whites, and blues of mountains, snowfields, and glaciers. The bay is peaceful, serene, and stunningly beautiful. The miles slip by effortlessly.

Perry heads toward a campsite on a grassy slope with commanding views up and down the fjord. Behind camp, tall snowy peaks stretch for the sky. A rocky stream tumbles cheerily down the grassy slope into the fjord. As we approach, a family of otters studies us, then disappears under the water. A bald eagle stares down at our strange vessels from a tall tree. We rig our ultra-tarp system, but tonight there is no need. The clear weather

holds and we stay dry all through the night, cooled by the chilled air sweeping down from the glaciers and snowfields above.

In the morning the waters of Blackstone Bay are once again glass-calm. We dodge bits of ice that hang motionless in the cold teal waters. There isn't a breath of wind stirring the surface. Although the sky is once again high overcast, there is no immediate threat of rain.

Our destination is Shotgun Cove, and after a leisurely day of paddling, with many stops to look around and drink in the beauty and silence, we find a campsite. High on a shingle beach, we have superb views north to the snowy Chugash Range, which rises high above Passage Canal. The next morning, our last in Prince William Sound, the water remains calm as we paddle back to Whittier. Soon we see the familiar sight of the concrete high-rise vying for attention with the glaciers behind the town. And then we are ashore, heading back to Anchorage.

There's a saying up here that "Anchorage is only a half hour from Alaska," and as we head toward the city we yearn for the snow-swept peaks and cobalt fjords of the sound. But as we round Beluga Point near Girdwood, our pangs for wilderness lost fade when we see two dozen or more beluga whales. The white whales blow and spout and play in the sun-dappled waters of Turnagain Arm.

A kayaker negotiates the brash ice at the foot of the Beloit Glacier in Prince William Sound.

139

PARADISE

Midway Atoll National Wildlife Refuge, Hawaii

THERE IS A DISTINCT SOUND that a big game fish makes when it hits a trolling lure. It's a deep, reverberating *ka-thunk* that sets people in motion as if a hand grenade had been lobbed in their midst. This sound suddenly reaches us over the roar of the powerful engines, and four heads snap toward it as one, four pairs of eyes scan the surface where the plastic squid had been skipping across the water just a moment before. And then all hell breaks loose. There's an explosion like a depth charge astern. One of the trolling rigs jerks with a crash, then doubles over violently, like a divining rod straining toward an artesian mother lode. Line zings off the reel with a sound that makes my blood race.

"Fish on!" yells crewman Mike Straight. With practiced motions he grabs the rod and leans back once, twice, striking hard to set the hook. "Big *ahi*. Steve, put on the belt!" I buckle on the fighting belt and Mike hands me the rod, then clears the five other trolling lines in a hurry. I jam the butt nock into the belt's gimbal cup just as the fish takes a hard run. *Zingggg.*

"Brace your thighs against the gunwale," Mike shouts over his shoulder. The ahi pulls me to my toes as the *Yorktown* slams into a roller. I almost go over the rail. I start to tighten the drag to slow the fish but catch myself. That's how big ones are lost. "Let him run," Mike orders as the reel sizzles. "Let him take all the line he wants. There's nothing you can do to stop him." The line shears through the water like a jigsaw, and for the next half hour the ahi, or yellowfin tuna—a torpedo of a fish, one of the fastest swimmers in the sea—takes run after blistering run. From time to time I catch a glimpse of something white flashing through the water like a tracer bullet, easily ripping off whatever line I had struggled to reel in. My biceps are burning when the beautiful fish finally rises like a phantom from the depths and is gaffed aboard.

Hawaiian spinner dolphins flash in and out of Midway Atoll's exquisite twenty-five square-mile turquoise lagoon.

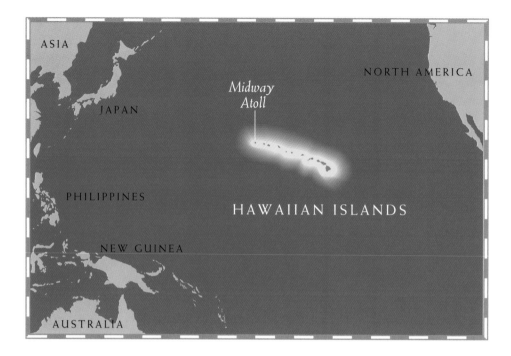

Twenty-foot rollers rush toward us from across the open ocean. From their peaks I can see Midway Atoll's sugary white beaches on the blue horizon. The tiny island looks adrift, lost at sea. Up in the steering console of the *Yorktown*, a thirty-eight-foot sportfishing boat, John Bone wrestles with the wheel as the vessel smashes through the heavy seas. The *Yorktown* lifts skyward as the waves roll under the hull, then slams down into the deep troughs. The boat is named for the World War II aircraft carrier that sank somewhere in these waters after taking three bombs and two torpedoes on a June day more than half a century ago.

On that day in 1942, the Imperial Navy of Japan launched a *Kido Butai*—a Carrier Strike Force—against Midway in a bold attempt to seize the atoll as a stepping-stone for attacks against Hawaii and the U.S. mainland. At the time, the U.S. Navy was still reeling from the devastating assault on Pearl Harbor six months earlier. For the Americans the situation was desperate. But the Yanks held one secret advantage: their intelligence officers had cracked the Japanese code, and that made all the difference.

Admiral Nagumo's strike force steamed into an ambush. In one of the greatest naval battles in history, American aircraft flew desperate sorties from airfields on Midway and from three aircraft carriers, the *Yorktown*,

Enterprise, and *Hornet.* Uncertain if they had enough fuel to return to base, American fliers crippled the Japanese fleet, sending four carriers, a heavy cruiser, 253 planes, and 3,500 pilots and sailors to the bottom. The Battle of Midway was Japan's last offensive, and it marked the turning point of the war in the Pacific.

If the vast Pacific is like the universe, its myriad islands like the stars burning bright in the midnight sky, then Midway Atoll is a tiny constellation at the far edge of the cosmos. Indeed, flying to Midway is as close to space travel as I've ever come.

The little nineteen-passenger Gulfstream turboprop jumped off the tarmac at Kauai's Lihue Airport at sunset, then gained altitude above the

fluted cliffs of the Na Pali coast. Through the large oval window I watched Niihau and then the little rock outcrop called Nihoa slide by under the wings. The sky turned a deep indigo and the powerful Rolls Royce engines hummed through the night as the plane worked its way up the Northwestern Hawaiian Islands, traveling from star to star. I followed our progress on the chart that Gail, the lone flight attendant, gave me and tried to memorize the fantastic names: Disappearing Island, La Perouse Pinnacle, French Frigate Shoals, Gardner Pinnacles, Laysan Island, Pearl and Hermes Reef. Beyond all of these, at the very edge of the chart, was a little speck: Midway, quite likely the most remote inhabited spot on earth.

These islands are the forgotten Hawaii, a galaxy of reefs, rocky outcrops, and sandy beaches stretching northwest across the Pacific for some 1,200 miles beyond Kauai, the most isolated of the main Hawaiian Islands. Little known, rarely visited, and for the most part uninhabitable, the Northwestern Hawaiian Islands have been off-limits to virtually everyone except military personnel and a handful of wildlife biologists for nearly a century.

From its discovery in 1859 through the early decades of the twentieth century, Midway Atoll was a place apart, a tiny strand of coral at the edge of the imagination. In 1903, President Theodore Roosevelt placed Midway under Navy jurisdiction to protect the atoll's seabird populations from Japanese plume hunters. Later that year, Roosevelt sent the first round-the-world telegraph message through a cable link on Midway. But it was the events of June

Golden light illuminates the seven-foot wingspan of an albatross gliding on early morning air currents.

4–6, 1942, that brought these obscure islets to the world's attention. From then on the atoll's strategic importance was not in doubt, and the U.S. maintained a strong military presence here throughout the Cold War.

Following the collapse of the Soviet Union and subsequent military cutbacks, the military's tenure ended in June 1997, when a skeleton crew of five Navy officers set sail from here for the last time. The necklace

of three low-lying coral islands and a frothy reef, all encircling an exquisite twenty-five-square-mile turquoise lagoon, was transferred from the military to the U.S. Fish and Wildlife Service (USFWS). In a groundbreaking arrangement, the USFWS subcontracted with private companies to provide wildlife-oriented recreation on the atoll.

Ironically, the Navy may have saved Midway's wildlife from the complex web of problems that has cost the main Hawaiian Islands more than 80 percent of their indigenous species, the most devastating loss of an archipelago's wildlife anywhere on earth. The atoll is home to the largest Laysan albatross colony and the second largest black-footed albatross colony in the world. Each year the diminutive atoll hosts an extravagant display of more than two million birds, including shearwaters, petrels, tropic birds, boobies, and terns. Perhaps most impressive are its great frigate birds, which hang in the sky for hours on end, barely changing positions, like stationary kites with eight-foot wingspans.

Each year the diminutive atoll hosts an extravagant display of more than two million birds, including shearwaters, petrels, tropic birds, boobies, and terns.

Midway is also one of the last refuges of the endangered Hawaiian monk seal and the threatened Pacific green sea turtle, as well as an important sanctuary for the Hawaiian spinner dolphin. The reef teems with some 266 species of fish, and the offshore waters are busy with blue marlin, Pacific sailfish, tuna, wahoo, and mahimahi.

As the Gulfstream droned through the night, I had an eerie feeling that I was speeding back through time. The airship itself spoke of a more romantic era, a time when air travel was still infused with a sense of adventure. The anachronistic sound of the propellers, the lavishly appointed cabin, even Gail with her prim blue skirt reaching well below her knees and her freshly starched white shirt, seemed out of place in the 1990s. I couldn't

shake the feeling that my fellow passengers and I had somehow boarded the ghost of the Pan American Clipper, the luxurious flying boat of the 1930s that stopped overnight on Midway to refuel en route to the Far East.

Five hours later, lights twinkled improbably in the blackness outside the aircraft. The Gulfstream steered towards them, then touched down and taxied to a cavernous hangar. It was 1:30 in the morning. Exiting the aircraft, I heard a chaotic whistling and screeching and clacking that rose from the darkness beyond the runway floodlights.

A figure stepped from the shadows and introduced herself as Barbara Maxfield, of the USFWS. She ushered me under a giant sign proclaiming *Naval Air Facility Midway*, past a brace of enormous ship anchors, and into the hangar, where I was assigned lodging. A few minutes later I settled into my room in Bravo Barracks, a former bachelor officer's quarters. I snapped off the light and fell asleep to the bizarre hullabaloo emanating from just outside my window.

The source of the strange noises was revealed the next morning when I opened my door onto the hallway and was greeted by an enormous bird with huge, webbed feet. This creature, which looked like a giant seagull,

Sparkling sunlight dances on the water as the boat crosses the shallow lagoon between Sand and Eastern Islands.

had the most piercing, intelligent eyes of any bird I have ever seen. It was an albatross, and I followed as it waddled down the long linoleum corridor and out the door into the bright sunshine, where it introduced me to thousands of its close friends and relatives.

"Incredible, isn't it?" asked Barbara. She had sidled up to me while I stood, dumbfounded, trying to comprehend the scene before me. There were albatross *everywhere*, tens of thousands of them. There were albatross wheeling in the sky on great seven-foot wings, albatross sitting on the nests that covered virtually every square foot of the island, albatross incubating huge eggs that looked like something out of *The Flintstones*. Strangest of all were the pairs of albatross performing their highly ritualized mating dance.

Two albatross approached each other with heads bobbing and weaving. After circling each other for a minute or so, the birds loudly clacked their beaks together, took turns bowing their heads and raising their wings, then pointed their beaks skyward and trumpeted their passion to heaven on high. But the music they made didn't sound like instruments; it sounded like cattle mooing.

"They don't have it quite down yet, but they're working at it," said Barbara approvingly.

After decades of coexistence, Midway's inhabitants, both human and wild, appear remarkably well adapted to one another.

She explained that these dancing birds were adolescents, back on Midway for the first time since hatching here seven years ago. Since they were fledglings they had wandered at sea, never touching land. Now they were back in the old neighborhood, navigating albatross society for the first time. It was bound to be awkward. But they would eventually find a mate for life, which could be sixty years or more, and together they would return to Midway every year.

I came to love these birds during my time on Midway. They had no fear, allowing me to crawl within a few inches before they turned that penetrating gaze upon me. In the evenings when I ran to Frigate Point, at the western tip of Sand Island, to catch the sunset, they lined the path by the thousands. The birds turned their heads and watched me pass, shrieking and whistling and clacking their beaks with applause as I ran by.

That first morning, Barbara and I jumped in a golf cart for a tour of Sand Island. We stopped first at a burned-out concrete building. In 1941, this hulk was the Navy's communication command post, a supposedly bombproof structure. On the night of December 7, 1941, Japanese destroyers *Ushio* and *Sazanami* were returning from the attack on Pearl Harbor when they decided to linger awhile and wreak some havoc on Midway.

Albatross make themselves at home in front of Bravo Barracks, a former U.S. Navy Bachelor Officer's Quarters that now lodges visitors to the atoll.

OVERLEAF:
There are albatross everywhere: wheeling in the sky, sitting on nests, and incubating huge prehistoric-looking eggs.

While Japanese planes strafed the airfield and burned the seaplane hangar, the warships lobbed hundreds of shells at the atoll. In a weird foreshadowing of the "smart bombs" used in the Gulf War, one of the shells snuck down an air shaft and blew up the impregnable post. First Lieutenant George Cannon became the first Medal of Honor winner of World War II, posthumously, when he refused medical treatment until the communications system was back on line. He died of his wounds later that night.

Midway is a last refuge for the highly endangered Hawaiian monk seal.

Other poignant reminders of the war are scattered throughout the two main islands. At the waterfront on Eastern Island, a rusting cannon guards the approach to the pier. On larger Sand Island, gun emplacements, ammunition bunkers, and the little armored pillboxes that each sheltered a single rifleman stand witness to the events of June 4–6, 1942.

During the Cold War, the atoll was a vital component of America's defense structure, with some 3,000 military personnel stationed here. In 1968 alone 313 ships and 11,077 aircraft stopped here on their way to and from Vietnam. In 1969, President Nixon and Vietnamese President Thieu held secret meetings in the Midway House halfway between their countries.

And then nothing. A rich past and no future. The next two decades saw a stream of departing servicemen, a diminishing strategic importance, and a shrinking share of the Pentagon budget. Finally, in 1993, the death knell rang in the form of a terse statement announcing that Naval Air Facility Midway was to be "operationally closed."

One night I joined my barracks mates, Dave and Ann, a cameraman and a producer from a Seattle television station, for a night on the town. We rode our Schwinn cruisers—1960s-style bikes with upright handlebars and front baskets—through the warm night, dodging albatross crossing the curvilinear streets of the base neighborhood. We rode to the All Hands Club, the former NCO bar where the diverse elements of Midway society gather after hours.

There are currently about 200 people living on Midway, mainly the Thais, Sri Lankans, and Filipinos who operate the island infrastructure, pilots and aircraft mechanics, adventure-travel company personnel, and the USFWS

folks. But it doesn't matter who you are or how long you've been there, whoever happens to be on the atoll is warmly absorbed into the community.

When Dave, Ann, and I walked through the wood-paneled doors of the
All Hands Club, we stepped back into the Age of Aquarius: the bar hadn't
changed since the Vietnam War. Creedence Clearwater Revival was blasting
on the jukebox. The mod mural might have been done by Peter Max. And
the prices listed behind the bar—Budweiser: fifty cents; Heineken: one
dollar—stopped us in our tracks. Suddenly feeling flush, I ordered a round
for the house.

"That will be $8.50," said Unni, the bartender. Big bucks in 1968.

The next day I caught a glimpse of Midway's future. Sparkling sunlight danced on the water as Larry Millwood, then owner of Midway Dive
& Snorkel—one of the companies subcontracted to handle adventure travel
on the atoll—piloted his forty-five-foot custom dive boat, the *Spinner D*,

*These feathered
creatures, which
looked like
enormous seagulls,
had the most
piercing, intelligent
eyes of any birds
I had ever seen.*

151

across the shallow lagoon. The water was like glycerin, so clear we could see every detail on the sandy bottom twenty, thirty feet down. Unfortunately, the winter currents were too powerful for diving, but Millwood told me all about what I was missing.

"This is diving's last frontier," he flatly declared. "The Caribbean has been done to death, and so has the rest of the Pacific. All the divers I talk to want a new challenge, unknown terrain, and that's what this place is all about.

"There are lots of shipwrecks waiting to be found on the outer reef, not to mention all these incredible coral heads in the lagoon," he pointed with his chin as the vessel passed above an expansive purplish mound rising like a balloon from the white sand bottom.

"But outside the reef is where the real excitement is," he continued. "Out there we've found these wild lava formations, all these tubes and weird overhangs. But what really blows me away is the fish traffic. It's real high energy, like standing in the middle of the freeway, watching all these uluas, jacks, snappers, rays, and reef sharks fly by." He paused, scanning the surface. "Hey, check out the spinners!"

About a quarter mile away the lagoon's resident pod of some 200 spinner dolphins spotted the boat and made a beeline for us. Soon the *Spinner D* had an escort of leaping, diving, corkscrewing dolphins. A dozen or so of the sleek gray swimmers rode the bow wave while others flashed in and out of the water. Leaping high into the air, they snapped off rolls and backflips. Some, like show-offs at a playground, spun three or four full revolutions before smacking down into the lagoon.

"These guys love to play," said Millwood, "and they're a *blast* to dive with."

There was something about John Bone that reminded me of Rick in *Casablanca*. There was a slight physical resemblance to Bogart, a penchant for turning up in out-of-the-way places, and a self-assurance that some might interpret as cockiness but which I found perfectly appropriate for this setting. A former Alaskan bush pilot who went on to fly jets for Delta, Bone is the owner of Midway Sport Fishing.

"This is a completely unexplored, untouched fishery," Bone was saying as he piloted the *Yorktown* out of the lagoon through Brooks Channel and

into the open ocean. Though we were sitting high up in the steering console, the big Pacific swells were towering above us. Down below, Mike Straight was setting up the trolling rigs, while Richard De Clerck, the Department of the Interior lawyer overseeing Midway's transfer from the Navy to the USFWS, gripped the rail with a determined look and white knuckles.

"These fish have never seen a hook," Bone shouted over the wind, looking perfectly composed as the waves batted us about. "It's like a Hemingway story from the twenties and thirties. Every day we come out here and explore a little more, but we never know what's going to come up over the rail!"

I flipped through the daily fishing log and found that what's been coming up have been big fish and lots of them. Uluas, or giant trevallies—true bulldogs of the fish world—have proven to be a mainstay: a world record 105-pounder was caught by one of the first visitors. Blue marlin weighing up to 850 pounds have been tagged and released. Inside the reef, salt-water fly fishers have been exploring the crystalline shallows of the lagoon from the open decks of the Glacier Bay catamarans in Bone's fleet,

With Midway Atoll lying on the horizon, Mike Straight casts for uluas from the deck of a catamaran.

hooking into trevally, amberjack, Pacific pompano, and gray reef sharks. Tiger sharks weighing upwards of 1,000 pounds have been seen cruising inside and outside the reef.

When I pointed this out Bone chuckled one of those Bogart chuckles. "The tigers are scared to death of the big uluas," he said wryly. "I tell you these fish are bruisers, and they're ready to rumble."

Suddenly we heard a loud *ka-thunk*. I slid down the ladder like a fireman and saw one of the trolling rigs jerking toward the water. I buckled on the fighting belt, Mike handed me the rod, and I began the fight of my fishing life.

At some point during my sojourn on Midway I realized that, were I an albatross, I would stake a claim to the grassy knoll overlooking the waterfront. Where warships had once been moored, these days the *Yorktown*, *Enterprise*, and *Spinner D* tug gently at their lines. There is always a fresh breeze soughing through the ironwood trees here, great seabirds circling endlessly in the sky, sometimes dolphins playing in the shallows and green sea turtles bobbing in the swells.

Many places on Midway inspire me, especially Frigate Point, with its lonely sweep of sand, but it is here at the eastern end of Sand Island that I feel the powerful resonance of the atoll's past blend with the positive energy of its future. This is where the wildlife, and the people who come to experience the wildlife, will meet. Sipping a tumbler of John's scotch in the cool evening air, listening to Mike, John, and Richard talk about the day's discoveries and tomorrow's possibilities, I lean back in my chair and put up my feet. Breakers smash on the outer reef with the sound of distant cannon fire.

"Tomorrow we'll rig the fly rods and set out in the catamarans," John is saying. "We'll explore the lagoon, hook you up with a big ulua, an amberjack, maybe even a pompano or two."

Who knows? I think. On Midway you can never tell what's going to come up over the rail.

I came to love these birds during my time on Midway. They had no fear, allowing me to crawl within a few inches before turning that penetrating gaze upon me.

I was greeted by an enormous bird with huge webbed feet. It was an albatross, and I followed as it waddled down the corridor and introduced me to its friends and relatives.

*The information outlined here is by no means
all you'll need to know before heading out into the
wilderness, but it will get you well on your way.
For further information about a particular area,
write or call the contact provided at the end of each
trip planner below.*

Maine Woods

THE JOURNEY Canoe routes in northern Maine are
virtually unlimited, and the tour described is but
one of many variations. The classic Allagash
Wilderness Waterway trip begins at Chamberlain
Lake and continues for nearly one hundred miles to
the village of Allagash near the Canadian border.
BEST TIME TO GO Late summer through early fall
is the best time for a canoe trip in the Maine
Woods. In late August and September the days are
warm and the nights are cool, the bugs are gone,
and the snows of winter are still a few weeks away.
ESSENTIAL CLOTHING AND EQUIPMENT Be prepared for cool, wet weather. A basic late-summer
outfit includes: a broad-brimmed hat, long-sleeved
cotton or light wool shirt, light cotton or wool
pants, and rubber-bottom, leather-top boots. Be
sure to bring shorts and T-shirts for pleasant days.
Pack extra warm wool or fleece layers and a complete set of raingear. For trips early in the season,
bring a headnet for those times when the biting
insects are especially active.

As a general rule on all canoe trips, put together
a small daypack with useful personal items such
as sunscreen, sunglasses, a camera and plenty of
film, a notepad, binoculars, maps and a compass,
matches, a water bottle, and a basic first-aid kit.
This daypack will be indispensable while in the
canoe and on day hikes and side trips.
SPECIAL ATTRACTIONS The Allagash River drains
one of the most remote, expansive, and undeveloped regions in the United States. A canoe trip in
the Maine Woods offers an excellent opportunity
for viewing wildlife—including moose, deer, black

bear, beaver, pine marten, bald eagles, osprey, and
many other species. In addition, the native brook
trout and lake trout fishing is superb.
FOR MORE INFORMATION Contact: Maine Bureau
of Parks and Recreation, State House Station 22,
Augusta, Maine 04333. 207-287-3821

Ten Thousand Islands, Florida

THE JOURNEY There are many canoe routes among
the mangrove islands of the Ten Thousand Islands.
The classic canoe route through the Ten Thousand
Islands is the Wilderness Waterway, a 99-mile
small-boat trail that winds through the marine
and estuarine regions of Everglades National Park
from Everglades City to Flamingo.
BEST TIME TO GO The best time to visit is mid-
December through mid-April, when the weather
is generally clear, the temperature moderate, and
the biting insects less abundant.
ESSENTIAL CLOTHING AND EQUIPMENT The south
Florida sun can be intense, and it's easy to ruin
your trip by getting sunburned on the first day.
The sun not only strikes down from above, but also
reflects up from the water surface, so it's important
to cover up as much as possible with light, loose
clothing and plenty of sunscreen. Wear polarized
sunglasses to protect your eyes and to be able to see
the fish swimming beneath the water's surface.

Plan to carry a gallon of water per person per
day in hard plastic containers. Raccoons can smell
fresh water and will chew through any soft-sided
water carriers.
SPECIAL ATTRACTIONS The Ten Thousand Islands
comprise one of the most remote and inaccessible
wilderness regions in the United States, and a
canoe journey here is an opportunity to spend time
interacting with an almost unimaginable profusion
of marine, terrestrial, and avian life.
FOR MORE INFORMATION Contact: Superintendent,
Everglades National Park, 40001 State Road 9336,
Homestead, Florida 33034. 305-242-7700

Boundary Waters Canoe Area Wilderness, Minnesota

THE JOURNEY With over 1,200 miles of canoe routes, tours in the Boundary Waters are virtually unlimited. Most paddlers begin their journey in the traditional "jumping off" towns of Ely or Grand Marais, Minnesota.

BEST TIME TO GO Late summer is the best time for a canoe trip in the Boundary Waters. In late August and September the temperature is moderate, the bugs are gone for the season, and winter snow is still a few weeks away.

ESSENTIAL CLOTHING AND EQUIPMENT Be prepared for cool, wet weather. A basic summer outfit includes: a broad-brimmed hat, long-sleeved cotton or light wool shirt, light cotton or wool pants, and rubber-bottom, leather-top boots. Be sure to bring shorts and T-shirts for pleasant days. Pack extra warm wool or fleece layers and a complete set of raingear. For trips early in the season bring a headnet to protect against biting insects.

As on all canoe trips, remember to take the daypack described in the Maine Woods trip planner.

SPECIAL ATTRACTIONS At over a million acres, the Boundary Waters Canoe Area is one of the largest units in the National Wilderness Preservation system. It contains hundreds of pristine lakes, miles of undeveloped rivers, and the largest virgin forests remaining east of the Rocky Mountains.

FOR MORE INFORMATION Contact: Supervisor, Superior National Forest, 8901 Grand Avenue Place, Duluth, Minnesota 55808. 218-626-4300

Missouri Breaks, Montana

THE JOURNEY The classic canoe journey through the Missouri River Breaks begins at Fort Benton and continues for 149 miles through a dramatic, austere gorge to James Kipp State Park.

BEST TIME TO GO Late summer through early fall is the best time to paddle the Missouri Breaks. In late August and September the ferocious heat of mid-summer is over, the days are generally pleasantly warm, and the nights are refreshingly cool.

ESSENTIAL CLOTHING AND EQUIPMENT Be prepared for weather extremes. In summer, temperatures can soar above 100 degrees Fahrenheit, while in spring and fall the thermometer dips well below freezing. A basic outfit includes: a broad-brimmed hat, long-sleeved cotton or light wool shirt, light cotton or wool pants, and either old sneakers or rubber-bottom, leather-top boots for negotiating the muddy river banks. Hiking boots will make exploring areas on shore much easier and safer. Be sure to pack shorts and T-shirts for warm days. A complete set of raingear will keep you dry on the occasional rainy day.

Be sure to pack the daypack described previously and plan to carry a gallon of water per person per day to last between the few available water sources in the Missouri Breaks.

SPECIAL ATTRACTIONS This 149-mile segment is the only major portion of the mighty Missouri River protected and preserved in its natural, free-flowing state. A National Wild and Scenic River component, the section flowing through the Breaks is also the finest, least-altered segment of the Lewis and Clark National Historic Trail.

FOR MORE INFORMATION Contact: River Manager, Bureau of Land Management, PO Box 1160, Lewistown, Montana 59457. 406-538-7461

Teton Crest, Wyoming

THE JOURNEY The classic Teton Crest Traverse starts on Teton Pass and ends by descending Cascade Canyon to Jenny Lake, at the northern end of the Cathedral Group. From there, a pleasant ski along Cottonwood Creek, at the foot of the Teton Range, will bring you back to the Teton Park Road at the Taggart Lake trailhead.

BEST TIME TO GO Late March to May is typically the best season for trips here because snow conditions are usually stable, the days are longer and sunnier, and the nights are warmer than they were earlier in the year.

ESSENTIAL CLOTHING AND EQUIPMENT The weather can change abruptly at high altitude in the northern Rockies, so dress in layers, bring high-quality wind and waterproof shell gear (both jacket and pants), and pack a lightweight down jacket for cool evenings in camp.

For skiing, sturdy telemark skis and boots are a must. Those not adept at free-heel skiing should bring alpine touring gear, which enables you to lock your heels during descents. Climbing skins are essential on the steeper climbs, but bring a selection of ski waxes for touring. Bring sunscreen, sunglasses, and a pair of goggles for snowy days.

In addition to basic winter camping gear, carry avalanche safety equipment: transceivers, probes, and shovels. Practice using these tools before setting out.

SPECIAL ATTRACTIONS In addition to reliable snow, a long season, and a multitude of options for day trips, special attractions of the Teton Crest Traverse include some of the finest high-mountain scenery in the world, accessed by a relatively easy ski route.

FOR MORE INFORMATION Contact: Superintendent, Grand Teton National Park, PO Box 170, Moose, Wyoming 83012. 307-739-3399

Beartooth Mountains, Wyoming / Montana

THE JOURNEY Rising beyond the northwest boundary of Yellowstone National Park, the Beartooth Mountains straddle the border between Montana and Wyoming. Largely above the tree line, this huge expanse of wild country provides infinite options for multi-day wilderness trips.

BEST TIME TO GO Winter is lengthy in the Beartooths, so the summer backpacking and fly-fishing season is compressed into July and August, when the days are long and the climate moderate. However, one should be prepared for cold and snow at any time of year.

ESSENTIAL CLOTHING AND EQUIPMENT Snowfields abound even in summer, and much of the range is at or above 10,000 feet, so be prepared for chilly weather. Dress in layers, and be sure to bring waterproof and windproof shell pants and jacket, and a warm pair of gloves and hat.

SPECIAL ATTRACTIONS The Beartooths are a stunningly beautiful range, the most heavily glaciated in the lower 48 states, and the wilderness wandering here is as good as it gets. More than 700 miles of hiking trails and 1,000 clear, cool alpine lakes make this a prime backcountry destination.

FOR MORE INFORMATION Contact: Supervisor, Gallatin National Forest, 10 East Babcock Avenue, PO Box 130, Bozeman, Montana, 59711. 406-587-6701

Escalante, Utah

THE JOURNEY The many canyons of the Escalante River present hikers with an extraordinary array of desert hiking possibilities. This is remote, wild country, where there are very few established hiking trails, so the trip possibilities are limited only by a hiker's imagination, time, and interests.

BEST TIME TO GO March through mid-June, September, and October are the best months to explore the canyons of the Escalante because the days are generally pleasantly warm, while the nights are refreshingly cool.

ESSENTIAL CLOTHING AND EQUIPMENT While desert summer days can be hot, in spring and fall be prepared for comfortably warm days and cool evenings. Dress in layers and bring a warm sleeping bag for chilly nights when the temperature dips, often well below freezing. Streams flow through many canyons, so plan on hiking with wet feet part of the time. Many hikers bring a pair of old sneakers for walking along the wet canyon floors. Be sure to bring sunscreen, sunglasses, and a broad-brimmed hat for bright sunny days.

SPECIAL ATTRACTIONS The Escalante was the last major river in the continental United States to be named, and a hiking trip here will bring you to some of the most remote, wild, and beautiful landscapes in the desert Southwest. The region is a natural geological showcase, containing striking arches, natural bridges, and cascading waterfalls.

FOR MORE INFORMATION Contact: Escalante Field Office, Bureau of Land Management, PO Box 225, Escalante, Utah 84726. 801-826-5499

Death Valley National Park, California

THE JOURNEY Death Valley is a land of paradox and contrast. Though much of the park is below sea level, the valley is surrounded by spectacular mountain ranges. It is possible to explore sand dunes, ghost towns, and snow-covered peaks all in the same day. And despite its foreboding name, Death Valley is home to some 1,000 species of plants, including many splendid wildflowers and marsh grasses.

BEST TIME TO GO Death Valley is one of the hottest places on earth, where temperatures of 120 degrees are common in summer. Be aware that ground temperatures in summer are usually 50 percent hotter than air temperatures. In such heat, emergency situations quickly become life-threatening. From November through March, however, the climate is mild, with high temperatures in the 60s and 70s.

ESSENTIAL CLOTHING AND EQUIPMENT In spring and fall be prepared for pleasantly warm days and mild evenings. Light, loose-fitting clothing is ideal for keeping cool and for protection from the sun. Bring along a fleece jacket for the evenings. Wear sturdy hiking boots, and bring sunscreen, sunglasses, and a broad-brimmed hat. If you head into the backcountry, be sure to carry at least a gallon of water per person per day.

SPECIAL ATTRACTIONS Diversity is the catchword for Death Valley, and a journey here will take you from the briny salt pans of the valley floor to the wildflowers and bristlecone pines of the high peaks of the Panamint Range. In between are forsaken mines, abandoned ranches, and ghost towns. A word of caution: the abandoned mines can be dangerous. Besides the imminent danger of collapse, in some places old explosives were left behind when the miners departed. Unless you are qualified, it's a good idea to stay out of the mines altogether.

FOR MORE INFORMATION Contact: Superintendent, Death Valley National Park, PO Box 579, Death Valley, California 92328. 760-786-2331.

Prince William Sound, Alaska

THE JOURNEY With an area of some 15,000 square miles, kayak routes in Prince William Sound are infinite. Many sea kayakers begin their trip in the port of Whittier, at the head of Passage Canal. From Passage Canal, most paddlers either head north to College Fjord or south to Blackstone Bay.

BEST TIME TO GO Late June through early August is generally the best time to go. By mid-August, you may expect the first winter storms to start rolling in off the Bering Sea.

ESSENTIAL CLOTHING AND EQUIPMENT Be prepared for cool, wet weather. Bring lots of warm layers, a complete set of raingear, a broad-brimmed hat, rubber boots, a full-coverage fly for your tent, and at least one large 10 × 12' tarp. Many paddlers also bring a mosquito headnet for those times when the bugs are especially bad.

Guide Perry Solomonson keeps an umbrella handy while kayaking, which provides him with a portable refuge from persistent rains during late season trips.

SPECIAL ATTRACTIONS Prince William Sound is home to numerous fjords as well as the greatest concentration of tidewater glaciers in Alaska, and the scenery is unsurpassed. In addition to sea kayaking, there are many opportunities for hiking; fishing for silver, pink, chum, and king salmon; whale watching; and picking abundant blueberries and salmonberries.

FOR MORE INFORMATION Contact: Supervisor, Chugach National Forest, 201 E. 9th Ave., Anchorage, Alaska 99501. 907-271-2599.

Midway Atoll, Hawaii

THE JOURNEY Midway Atoll is one of the most isolated spots on earth. Located at the far western end of the Hawaiian chain, Midway comprises three small islands: Sand, Eastern, and Spit. There is much to see and do on the islands, and the opportunities for underwater diving, sport fishing, and nature and history study are unequaled.

BEST TIME TO GO Diving is excellent from April through November; fishing is best from March through November; and albatross nest on the atoll from November through July.

ESSENTIAL CLOTHING AND EQUIPMENT The sun can be strong on Midway Atoll during spring, summer, and fall. In the warm weather months, heavy-duty sunscreen and a wide-brimmed hat are crucial. Don't forget polarized sunglasses for looking though the water at coral formations and for spotting fish. Binoculars are useful for observing the abundant wildlife. Pack a light windbreaker and a fleece pullover for cool mornings and evenings. Be sure to bring a comfortable pair of low-cut hiking shoes for walking on the beaches and historic airfields.

SPECIAL ATTRACTIONS Midway Atoll National Wildlife Refuge is the only remote island refuge in the Pacific open to the general public. The atoll is a natural and historical treasure chest, including unsurpassed wildlife resources and remnants from one of the most decisive battles of World War II.

FOR MORE INFORMATION Contact: U.S. Fish and Wildlife Service, Pacific Islands Ecoregion, 300 Ala Moana Blvd., Box 50088, Honolulu, Hawaii 96850. 808-541-1201

ACKNOWLEDGMENTS

MANY THANKS TO THOSE who appear in this book in words or images, especially Mary Gorman, Dan Berns, Jay Pistono, Doc and Lee Dominick, and Garrett and Alexandra Conover. I appreciate the company and the friendship, the encouragement and inspiration, and the chance to share the American wilderness experience with you.

Profound thanks also to my valued colleagues, especially Charles Miers and Margaret Braver at Universe Publishing for their belief in and support of this project; Russell Hassell for his beautiful design work on this volume; Joel Hecker for his wise council; David Quammen for his advice, encouragement, and thoughtful foreword; and John Atwood, Tim Bogardus, and Bethanie Deeney at *Sports Afield* for all the times they've sent me back out to the American wilderness. Thanks also to Rob Center and Kay Henry at the Mad River Canoe Company for generously supplying the watercraft that appear in many of these pages.

Finally, thanks to my family, especially Mary and Tasha; my parents, Margaret and David Gorman; my sister, Liz, and her husband, Mark Kritzman; and also to my many treasured friends.